Read & Grow Rich

I N T I
PUBLISHING & RESOURCE BOOKS

Read and Grow Rich
How the Hidden Power of Reading Can
Make You Richer in All Areas of Your Life!

By Burke Hedges

Printed in the United States of America

ISBN: 1-891279-00-9
Published by INTI Publishing & Resource Books, Inc.
Tampa, FL
www.intipublishing.com
Cover design by Laurie Winters
Layout by Bayou Graphics

Famous People Who Have Read and Grown Rich!

Some good book is usually responsible for the success of every really great man.
—Roy L. Smith

- **Lou Holtz**, one of the winningest coaches in college football history, credits *The Magic of Thinking Big* as a turning point in his professional career

- **W. Clement Stone**, multi-millionaire businessman and best-selling author, says that Napoleon Hill's *Think and Grow Rich* "changed the course of my life." Hill's book inspired Stone to begin a lifelong habit of helping others by giving them personal growth books, a habit he followed religiously for 50 years.

- **Donna Reed**, Academy Award winner and early TV star, was a shy, insecure high school freshman when she read *How to Win Friends and Influence People*. Upon completing the book, she landed a lead role in the school play, setting the stage for a 40-year career in movies and TV.

- **J.W. Marriott**, president of Marriott Hotels, was so moved by the message of *The Greatest Salesman in the World* that he gives a copy to each of his marketing executives.

- **Dave Thomas**, founder of Wendy's Restaurants, was a high school dropout with a poor self concept when he happened to read *The Power of Positive Thinking*. Today he heads up a fast-food empire with thousands of restaurants all over the world.

- **Phyllis Diller**, the famous comedienne, was a frustrated, insecure housewife when she read *The Magic of Believing*. The book gave her the confidence to try her hand at show business, and she went on to become one of the best-known comics in the country.

- **Archie Moore**, the former light-heavyweight boxing champion who knocked out a record 141 opponents in 228 bouts, wasn't much of a reader until he was cast as the slave Jim in the movie version of *The Adventures of Huckleberry Finn*. Moore read the book to prepare himself for the part and from then on became an avid reader, saying, "Now that I've found books, I'm really living."

Dedication

This book is dedicated to my wife, Debbie, and to our four children—Burke, Jr., Nathen, Spencer, and Aspen Marie. Because of you, my life grows richer in love every minute of every day.

Also By Burke Hedges

- *Who Stole the American Dream?*

- *You Can't Steal Second with Your Foot on First!*

- *You, Inc.*

- *Copycat Marketing 101*

From the Desk of Burke Hedges

Reading Levels the Playing Field

In this book you're going to read about dozens of people from all backgrounds.

Some were born with a silver spoon in their mouths. Others were born on the wrong side of the tracks.

Some came from broken homes. Others grew up with two loving, nurturing parents.

Some were born with near-genius IQs. Others were born with average intelligence, at best.

Some were born handsome or pretty. Others were plain or even ugly.

Some were born free. Others to slavery.

Some were black... some were white... some were men... some were women... and on and on.

But every single person featured in these pages has one thing in common: They all dramatically improved their lives by reading.

You see, reading, like no other single activity, levels the playing field of life, so to speak. It's the great equalizer. Reading transforms us from who we are right now... to who we can become in the future. And when we're transformed even slightly, we're richer than we were the day before.

It's my sincere hope that this book will ignite your passion for reading, which, in turn, will empower you to discover your special talents and then use those talents to become all you can be.

Burke Hedges

Contents

Acknowledgments

To Dr. Steve Price, thank you for your tireless research, unwavering dedication, unique blend of talents, and unselfish commitment to INTI Publishing & Resource Books. You've been a great partner over the last seven years, but more than that, you've been a great friend. Again, many thanks for the many contributions you've made in years past—and, I'm sure, will continue to make in the years ahead.

To Katherine Glover, President of INTI Publishing and Resource Books, a special appreciation for your enthusiasm and attention to the details throughout the writing and editing process. Katherine, you autograph with excellence every project you touch. Thank you for your enormous contribution. You're one of the few people who walks the walk when it comes to reading and growing rich.

To Sandra Bailey, much appreciation for watching over my other business obligations while I invested the time to writing this book. I appreciate you more than you'll ever know.

To Sandee Lorenzen, Debbie Hedges, Jewel Parago, Linda Burleson, and Kim Plavnick, a long overdue "thank you" for taking care of the day-to-day operations of INTI Publishing. You're all special people, and you're definitely special to me.

To Pat Chrinko, Joel Bailey, Nancy Kevorkian, Jeff Keller, Ann Matherlee, and Shari Palasti, a big "thanks" for your suggestions and insights while this book was still a working manuscript.

Finally, I'd like to extend my heartfelt gratitude to each and every person who had a hand in this project. May your dedication and hard work come back to you a thousand fold, for your efforts will truly make a difference in someone's life.

INTRODUCTION

The Right Book at the Right Time Can Change Your Life!

> *A good book contains more*
> *real wealth than a good bank.*
> —Roy L. Smith

I'M LIVING PROOF THAT the right book at the right time can dramatically change your life.

Less than 12 years ago I was earning $5.50 an hour... sharing a tiny, one-bedroom apartment with my pregnant wife and our one-year-old son... driving a rusted-out 1976 red Datsun patched all over with gray fiberglass... feeling sorry for myself... disgusted with my job and my life... and not knowing what to do about it.

One day my sister-in-law—fed up with my complaining and sensing potential in me that even I didn't recognize—handed me a copy of Og Mandino's *The Greatest Salesman in the World.*

It was the turning point of my life.

Mandino's book inspired me to quit my dead-end job

and to seek a position selling cellular phones. Within a year of my first sale, I had opened my own cellular phone business, and, I'm proud to say, I've been a successful entrepreneur ever since.

I still shake my head in amazement when I think how my life has been enriched in so many ways by a paperback book costing less than $10!

Read and Grow Rich

The title of the book you hold in your hands is a tribute to Napoleon Hill's perennial best-seller, *Think and Grow Rich*, a wonderfully insightful book that has enriched my life—and the lives of millions of others—beyond all measure.

> *By reading we discover our world, our history, and ourselves.*
> —Daniel J. Boorstin

Hill's book, *THINK and Grow Rich*, explains how average people can grow rich financially by following the wealth-building principles learned from America's greatest industrialists, such as Andrew Carnegie, John D. Rockefeller, and Henry Ford.

This book, *READ and Grow Rich*, explains how the hidden powers of reading can empower you to *grow rich in the largest sense of the word*. Rich in money, yes. But also rich in love. Rich in happiness. Rich in family. Rich in health. Rich in fulfillment. Rich in your relationship with God. In other words, rich in all phases of your life.

Reading, more than any other activity, has the power to unlock our potential and, in the process, unleash the "better angels of our nature," to use a favorite phrase of Abraham Lincoln, an avid reader who dramatically transformed himself from a poor, backwoods boy to perhaps our greatest president through the power of the written word.

The Awesome Power of Reading

I've thought a lot about the impact *The Greatest Salesman in the World* and other great books have had on my life, trying to figure how black letters printed on a white piece of paper had the power to change the direction of my life. I've always known that something magical happened when I read, but for the longest time I couldn't put it into words. I just know that when I read good books, I experience something transforming... uplifting... and life-altering.

Then one day I came across an article by the Pulitzer Prize-winning historian Daniel J. Boorstin that summed up the value of reading in one simple, yet profound, sentence:

> By reading we discover our world, our history, and
> ourselves.

That quote pretty much explains the awesome power of reading. More than any other mental activity, reading changes and improves us by forcing us to think... to imagine... to examine... to grow... and in the process, "to discover our world, our history, and ourselves."

When we read inspiring, thought-provoking books, we grow richer in all phases of our lives. In short, reading has the power to transform us from what WE ARE right now to what WE COULD BE in the future. In the words of Henry David Thoreau, "A truly great book teaches me better than to read it. I must soon lay it down, and commence living on its hint... What I began by reading, I must finish by acting."

What You Will Learn in This Book

Reading influences us in ways we can't even comprehend. Research proves that reading changes the way humans solve problems, store information, tell stories, interpret the world, and think about ourselves. Reading even changes the shape of our brains! When we stop to really think about the impact that reading has on our lives, we're left standing in awe.

In the coming pages I'm going to help you better understand the powerful influence that reading plays in our culture and in our personal lives. You'll learn why the invention of reading and writing is still the greatest technological breakthrough in the history of the world. You'll learn what happens inside our minds when we read. You'll learn why literate cultures out-produce oral cultures. You'll learn why reading is different—and in many ways superior—to listening to the radio or watching TV. You'll learn how to read a book so that you get the most out of it. You'll learn why "e-books" will soon become as common as e-mail. And you'll learn why everyone—including YOU—can read and grow rich.

Get Reading and Get Growing

Whether you are an avid reader or whether this is the first book you have read since high school, the fact remains that this book—or perhaps the next book you pick up—can empower you to grow rich in a multitude of ways.

Growing rich starts with one simple, powerful act. You must pick up a book... open it... and start reading... so that you can start growing in ways you never imagined before.

1

Seven Years Later...

*Many times the reading of a book has
made the future of a man.*
            —Ralph Waldo Emerson

IT'S A MAGNIFICENT, CLEAR, sunny day in late March, 1993, and my wife, Debbie, and I are standing on top of the mountain in Aspen, Colorado. We can see for miles and miles in all directions. I press forward into my ski boots and lean against my ski poles, calmly surveying the vast, white beauty that surrounds me.

"*I feel so blessed,*" I say to myself as the sun glistens off the fresh powder beneath my skis. "Why me? What did I do to deserve all this?"

I'd planned this short ski vacation to Aspen as a surprise present for my wife, who had been traveling with me on a business trip to Arizona. Before heading to Arizona, I'd gathered up Debbie's ski clothes one morning while she was out running errands and arranged to have them shipped to the Ritz Carlton in Aspen. I had my secretary schedule our return flight through Denver and book a private plane to Aspen, where a limo driver from the Ritz would be waiting.

Debbie was caught totally off guard! When we boarded the flight in Denver, she was convinced we were heading back to Florida! It wasn't until we were enjoying a great meal in first class that I let her in on my secret—we were heading for Aspen for a much-deserved five-day vacation! Debbie was surprised. And delighted. And we had a terrific vacation that we'll both remember and cherish for the rest of our lives.

Why Am I So Blessed?

A light snow drifted soundlessly to the ground as I rested at the top of Aspen Mountain, pondering the questions, *"Why me?... What did I do to deserve all this beauty and luxury?"*

My mind flashed back to 1986, when my sister-in-law handed me *The Greatest Salesman in the World.* At the time, I was in debt, out of shape, and nearly out of hope. Up to that point in my life, I'd never been a big reader. Oh, sure, I'd read my share of textbooks and short stories for school assignments, but I'd never read a "personal growth" book before in my life. But for some reason, I was drawn to Mandino's book.

> *Books are for nothing but to inspire.*
>
> —Ralph Waldo Emerson

I remember that as I thumbed through the pages, my eyes came to rest on a page with the headline "Scroll 1: *Today I begin a new life.*"

"Looks interesting. Thanks, Susan," I said as I tossed the book onto the dining room table. "I'll start it today." Later that afternoon I picked up the book and plopped down on our lumpy, second-hand couch to read.

"I'll read a few pages before turning on the football game," I thought to myself. "It's a pretty skinny book... it should be easy enough to finish before I see Susan again."

It was easy to finish, all right. I read *The Greatest Salesman in the World* in one sitting. I still remember how the book moved me to tears and gave me hope for a better life: "If an uneducated camel boy can rise from poverty to great wealth by following the principles in this book, then so can I," I thought.

·········

I LOWERED MY SKI GOGGLES over my eyes to cut down on the blinding glare. It was early in the day, so I was in no hurry to head down the mountain. I chose to savor the moment a little longer, and to ponder how much my life had changed over the last seven years... and to think how differently things might have turned out if I had chosen not to read that small paperback book.

Sentences are like sharp nails which force truth upon our memory.

—Diderot

"Choice. What an amazing concept," I thought as I watched a steady stream of skiers choose their paths down the mountain. "That guy in the yellow ski suit is choosing to hug the tree line. That heavy-set guy is choosing to traverse the mountain in a long, slow line. And that teen-ager is choosing to charge straight down the hill. Every skier on this hill is trying to accomplish the same goal—to get safely to the bottom of the mountain and to have fun in the process. But they are all choosing different paths to get there."

Suddenly two members of the ski patrol swerved past me, pulling a sled with an injured skier.

"That guy chose to zig when he should have zagged, and boom, his life heads in a direction he never anticipated. All of our choices, big ones and small ones alike, have consequences. It's the law of cause and effect," I thought as I watched the injured skier gradually dissolve into the distance.

Choice, Not Chance, Determines Your Destiny

When I chose to read *The Greatest Salesman in the World*, I had no idea at the time how it would change my life. At the time it seemed like such a small, inconsequential choice. But like the injured skier who chose to "zig instead of zag," small choices can have enormous consequences. Even a seemingly small choice, like deciding to join a fitness center or putting on your seat belt before you pull out of the driveway, can dramatically change the direction of your life.

It was easy to read *The Greatest Salesman in the World*. I finished it in a couple of hours, tops.

But it would have been just as easy NOT to read it.

I could have easily glanced at the book as I walked past it

and chose to put off reading it for another day... and then another day... and another day... until it was just one more "chore" that I never quite got around to doing.

But I had the good sense—and the good fortune— to use my God-given ability to make a choice that would help me rather than hurt me.

My good friend Gary Blair, author of *What Are Your Goals?*, closes all of his correspondence with these words: "Everything Counts." One day I asked him what he means when he says, "everything counts."

"It means that everything you do, no matter how big or how small, is either taking you closer to your goals or further away from them. That's why everything counts."

That statement is so simple, yet so profound. Everything counts! It's true! Our choices are either helping us get better or holding us back. There is no middle ground. Everything counts.

I wasn't consciously thinking that "everything counts" years ago when I chose to read *The Greatest Salesman in the World*, but deep down inside I must have been aware that big changes start with little choices. At the time I was so fed up with my life that I was determined to do whatever it took to make some big changes. If that meant choosing to read a book, then that's what I was willing to do. Like I said, it's one of the best choices I've ever made.

Transformed by the Written Word

You've probably heard the old expression, "When the student is ready, the teacher will appear." That expression was certainly true for me in 1986—I was the student and Og Mandino was the teacher.

Ironically, when I started reading his book, I had no idea how it would impact my life. I certainly didn't expect to be changed. Entertained, yes. Changed, no.

But as I turned the pages, I could feel something almost magical happening to me. It was as if someone inside me... a more sensitive, deeper, more honest, more open me- -the INNER ME, if you will—was reading the book. And the "inner me" was listening to the message with an open heart and a willing mind.

Before I tell you what it was that spoke so directly to me, please allow me to recap the plot, just in case you haven't read the book yet. The story of *The Greatest Salesman in the World* takes place 2,000 years ago in Palestine near the village of Nazareth. An elderly, wealthy merchant named Hafid, known to all as "The Greatest Salesman in the World," tells his trusted servant the story of how he rose from poverty to become fabulously wealthy.

> *Reading is a means of thinking with another person's mind: It forces you to stretch your own.*
>
> —Charles Scribner, Jr.

The plot is clever and suspenseful, and I won't spoil the book for you by telling you the details. But a large part of the book concerns 10 ancient scrolls, each containing a timeless success principle. They are as follows:

Scroll   1:   *Today I begin a new life*
Scroll   2:   *I will greet this day with love in my heart*
Scroll   3:   *I will persist until I succeed*
Scroll   4:   *I am nature's greatest miracle*
Scroll   5:   *I will live this day as if it were my last*
Scroll   6:   *Today I will be master of my emotions*
Scroll   7:   *I will laugh at the world*
Scroll   8:   *Today I will multiply my value a hundredfold*
Scroll   9:   *I will act now*
Scroll 10:   *Henceforth I will pray, but my cries for help will be cries for guidance.*

As you can see, the principles have more to do with living a happy, fulfilled life than they do with selling, per se, but that's one of Mandino's points: Selling is life, and life is selling.

....

AS I STOMPED MY SKIS into the snow, small crusts of ice sprayed off my boots in all directions. I took a deep breath and exhaled slowly, savoring the moment.

"It doesn't get any better than this," I said to myself. I felt so relaxed and so content. I was in no hurry for this moment to end.

"Why don't you ski on down to the lodge?" I said to Debbie.

"I'll join you in a few minutes for a hot chocolate."

I watched Debbie make her way down the hill, her long, dark hair flowing behind her. My mind kept returning to *The Greatest Salesman in the World* as I struggled to recall what it was about the book that motivated me to improve my life and, in the process, the lives of my wife and my growing family.

One word kept popping up over and over in my mind: hope.

A truly great book teaches me better than to read it. I must soon lay it down, and commence living on its hint...What I began by reading, I must finish by acting.

—Henry David Thoreau

The book gave me hope that if Hafid, a poor camel boy, could become rich, then I, Burke Hedges, a poor boat builder, could do the same. The book gave me hope that success was attainable by almost anyone who was willing to learn and apply a few simple, timeless principles spelled out in an inexpensive paperback book.

I've sat through a lot of lectures in a lot of classrooms during my lifetime. Got a college degree in criminal justice to prove it. But not one single teacher in my 16 years of formal schooling ever taught me one single thing about success principles. As I read and re-read the principles on each scroll, Mandino-the-author became Mandino-my-mentor.

Within two weeks of reading *The Greatest Salesman in the World*, I resigned from my job and applied for a new job selling cellular phones. I had no sales experience when I applied for the job. I remember sitting in the parking lot at 5:30 in the morning waiting for the manager to open up. I literally had to beg the guy to give me the job that paid $250 a week plus commissions. He had so little faith in me that he assigned me to a rural territory, 45 miles from our apartment. Two hours of my day was wasted driving to and from work.

But I was determined to succeed, no matter what! I faithfully followed the principles set down by Mandino over and over again—"I will persist until I succeed; Today I will multiply my value a hundredfold; I will act now"—and I started getting immediate results. By the end of the first month, I'd earned $4,000 in commissions. By the end of the second month, I was the leading salesman in the district. And within a year, I had opened my own cellular phone business.

I'll admit that I may not have become the greatest salesman in the world. But I was on my way to becoming the best that I could be. I was, indeed, growing rich in all areas of my life.

Questions Led to Writing This Book

During and after that Aspen vacation, I've spent a lot of time thinking about Mandino's book and the scores of other books I've read since then. Here are a few of the key questions I kept asking myself:

- Where would I be today if I hadn't chosen to read *The Greatest Salesman in the World*?
- What is it about books that enables them to strike such deep chords within us?
- What other books have profoundly affected my life?
- Have other people had their lives changed by books? If so, which people and which books?
- Is there something unique about reading that makes it an especially powerful agent of change?
- Is there a positive correlation between success and reading?
- Would the world be a drastically different place today if reading had never been invented?

I've researched these questions, and scores of others, over the years. The answers to these questions eventually became the book you're holding in your hands.

Up to this point you've read about how a book changed my life.

Before we talk about how a book can change your life, let's take a few moments to read some amazing rags-to-riches stories about struggling people—many of whom later became famous—who transformed their lives through the power of reading, proving once and for all that people can, indeed, read and grow rich!

2

The Power of Books to Transform Lives

> *Every man who knows how to read*
> *has it in his power to magnify himself,*
> *to multiply the ways in which he exists,*
> *to make his life full, significant, and*
> *interesting.*
>
> —Aldous Huxley

A SOCIOLOGIST WRITING a textbook couldn't invent a better case study of a family destined for disaster than that of Sonya Carson and her two young sons, Curtis and Ben. Statistically speaking, the boys stood a better chance of going to prison than graduating from high school.

Sonya spent her childhood being shuffled from one foster home to another. She rarely attended school, and at age 13 she married an older man, unaware that he already had a wife and five children.

Shortly after she gave birth to her second son, her husband deserted her, and Sonya sank into such a deep depression that she had to be hospitalized in a suicide-prevention ward. Dirt poor and living in a run-down public housing project in one of the meanest sections of Baltimore,

Sonya and her two boys were seemingly doomed to a life of crime, drugs, and despair.

Read & Grow Rich in the Ghetto

But Sonya, despite her lack of formal education, was determined that her boys would succeed. For starters, she limited them to watching two TV programs a week. The rest of their spare time, she announced, would be spent reading.

Sonya insisted the boys read books and submit book reports to her every week, requiring the boys to read them aloud to her because she could barely read herself. She also required her sons to read to her from her favorite book—the *Book of Proverbs*—and then explain to her what they had read.

All that Mankind has done, thought, gained, or been is lying in the pages of Books.

—Carlyle

It wasn't long before the boys were doing so well in school that they became ashamed of their mother. They would say, "Mom, why can't you read better or talk better?" And Sonya would reply, "Teach me. If you can't teach me, don't criticize me."

By the time college came around, Sonya didn't have to worry about paying for tuition—both of her sons received college scholarships from major universities. Curtis graduated from the University of Michigan and Ben from Yale. Sonya always believed the American Dream could best be accomplished through education, so she decided to practice what she preached. She, too, returned to school, earning her GED while the boys were getting their college degrees.

With her sons' help, Sonya improved her reading and writing skills: "I would write papers and ask them to correct me," she recalls. With her new education, Sonya was able to leave behind a string of menial jobs and become an interior decorator.

The boys went on to enjoy professional careers. Curtis is an engineer and his wife is a physician. His brother, Dr. Benjamin Carson, is the director of pediatric neurosurgery at Johns Hopkins Hospital and author of the best-selling book *Think Big!*

The Carson's are proof that the written word has the power to transform lives. If the Carson family can read and grow rich despite the overwhelming odds they faced, just think what the average family can do!

Books: They're Right in Front of Our Faces!

You know, when I hear stories like the one about the Carson family, it reminds me of one of Peter Drucker's key success principles—"see the obvious." It's so *obvious* that people who are avid, life-long readers get ahead in life, and that the people who aren't... well, let's just say that minimum readers earn minimum wages—or worse!

Statistics from the National Institute for Literacy prove this out:

- 75% of unemployed adults have reading and writing difficulties
- 43% of adults with low literacy skills live in poverty (as compared with 5% of those with high literacy skills)
- 22% of American adults—40 million people—read and write at the fifth grade level or below
- 70% of prisoners score in the two lowest literacy levels

These are some pretty depressing statistics, and they confirm the *obvious*: People who can't read (or won't read) in the Information Age will grow poor while we readers grow rich!

Self-Imposed Illiteracy

I'm concerned about the problem of "functional illiteracy" in this country, so much so that a portion of the profits from the sale of this book will be donated to fighting illiteracy.

But I'm more concerned about "self-imposed illiterates," that is, people who *can read* very well, but, for whatever reason, are *choosing NOT to read* or people who are wasting their time reading junk, like gossip magazines and weekly tabloids. As Mark Twain observed, "The person who can read but doesn't isn't any better off than the person who can't read."

Frankly, I think Mark Twain is being too kind. I think the person who can read but doesn't is WORSE OFF than the person who can't read because they're taking a special gift for granted.

> *I cannot live without books.*
>
> —Thomas Jefferson

Choosing to remain a self-imposed illiterate would be like being handed a winning lottery ticket and being too lazy to stop to the bank and cash it in. If you're anything like me, you'd *make the time* to get by the bank! Same thing goes for improving yourself—you have to *make the time to read*.

You know, it wasn't that long ago in our country's history that the majority of adults were illiterate. From 1776 until 1900, most Americans lived on farms or in small cities, and a strong back was a lot more useful and valuable than a strong education when it came time to clear the land and bring in the crops.

But as the old saying goes, "Where there's a will, there's a way," and a few determined pioneers—such as Abraham Lincoln—and resourceful slaves—such as Frederick Douglass—overcame seemingly insurmountable odds to learn how to read. Reading not only changed their lives— it changed the course of history!

Books and the Making of a President

Abraham Lincoln was born in a one-room cabin in rural Kentucky, and his formal schooling added up to less than a year. His mother could read but had never learned to write, and his father could write his name and not much else.

But Lincoln was fascinated with books. He learned his ABCs while attending school a couple of days a week when he was seven, and he practiced writing his letters on hand-planed boards using the burned end of a stick as his "pencil." In the evenings he read the Bible aloud to his mother, and he read and re-read *Aesop's Fables* so many times that he memorized many of the stories.

As a teen-ager he sought out and borrowed books from every neighbor within 50 miles, including *The Autobiography of Benjamin Franklin*, *The Life of Washington*, and *Pilgrim's Progress*. Lincoln would read every chance he got. While the other youngsters played tag in the hills, young Abe was sitting under a tree with a book in his hand. When he took lunch breaks from splitting rails, he'd read while the others caught a catnap.

Lincoln's beloved mother died when he was only nine, and he and his older sister took solace by reading his mother's favorite passages from the Bible. When his father remarried, the new bride, Sarah Bush Lincoln, brought a few pieces of furniture and three books to her new household: *Webster's Speller*, *The Adventures of Robinson Crusoe*, and *The Arabian Nights*. The young Lincoln read them over and over, and he became such a proficient speller that neighbors would pay him to write letters and simple wills for them.

College of Hard Knocks

When 21-year-old Lincoln struck out on his own, he eventually settled in New Salem, Illinois, a pioneer village of 100 settlers located on the edge of the western frontier. It was a blessing in disguise. New Salem boasted six men with college educations, including two widely read physicians, and they freely shared their books with Lincoln.

During the next seven years, Lincoln worked at two jobs that allowed for long stretches of uninterrupted reading, first as a clerk in a general store and later as a postmaster. He would occupy the down time between customers by reading widely in philosophy, science, religion, literature, law, and politics. In effect, *he gave himself a first-rate college degree by reading*, and in 1837, 28-year-old Abraham Lincoln was certified to practice law in the state of Illinois even though he had less than a first grade education!

By all accounts, Abraham Lincoln was smart, but he was far from a genius. He wasn't a speed reader with a photographic memory. He was more methodical than brilliant, oftentimes writing out passages word for word so that he could remember them and understand them more fully.

What Lincoln lacked in intellect he made up for in common sense and determination. He understood early in his life that reading was the best tool available for advancing in the world, and he transformed himself from a poor, undereducated backwoodsman into one of the greatest men in history through the amazing power of reading.

The Education of a Slave

At about the same time young Abe Lincoln was learning his ABCs in a rural schoolhouse, a 10-year-old slave named Frederick Douglass was learning his ABCs by listening as the wife of a plantation owner read stories to her young daughter. The plantation master was furious when he discovered one of his slaves was learning to read, and he demanded that his wife stop reading to their daughter while Douglass was around for fear reading would put thoughts of freedom into his head.

How right he was!

Slave owners fully understood the transforming power of reading, and they took measures to keep blacks powerless by keeping them illiterate. The southern states passed laws known as the "black codes," which outlawed educating slaves. In South Carolina, white citizens who taught blacks to read could receive six months in jail and a $100 fine. The state law recommended 10 lashes with a leather whip as punishment for slaves who were caught reading or attempting to learn to read. The recommended punishment for repeat offenders was to chop off the first knuckle of the index finger.

Douglass was aware of the black codes, but he defied them, for he, too, understood the power of the written word. Once the door to reading was opened a crack, Douglass forced it open the rest of the way. He practiced writing his ABCs on fences and walls with chalk. He borrowed books from the overseer's children and playmates, and read every spare moment. When he was 17, he acquired a copy of the *Columbian Orator*, a collection of speeches from famous orators about freedom and liberty. Douglass taught himself to write by copying the speeches over and over in longhand, and in the process he memorized long, eloquent passages that he would recite in later years at abolitionist rallies.

From Slave to Freedom Fighter

At age 21, Douglass disguised himself as a sailor and escaped to New York, where he was often invited to speak at anti-slavery fund-raisers. He continued filling in the gaps in his education by reading widely in litera-ture, philosophy, religion, and politi-cal science.

But as far as the law was concerned, he was still the property of his slave master, and Douglass, fearing he would be kidnapped and returned to his owner, escaped to England with his wife. He lectured in England for two

> *I believe that the book still is the primary carrier of ideas.*
>
> —George Will

years, eventually earning enough money from speaking fees and abolitionist sympathizers to return to America and pur-chase his freedom.

Douglass became one of the leading spokesmen for abol-ishing slavery and advancing women's rights, and for several decades he published *The North Star*, an abolitionist newspa-per with the slogan. "Right is of no sex—Truth is of no color—God is the Father of us all, and all we are Brethren."

History is filled with stories of men and women from humble backgrounds who have transformed themselves into world leaders through reading. The stories of Lincoln and Douglass are especially inspiring because of the struggles they faced in learning to read. But, thankfully, most of us modern-day Americans don't have to make heroic efforts to learn to read—we just have to take better advantage of our good for-tune instead of taking it for granted.

Let's take a brief look at some other famous people who used reading to maximize their full potential and transform their lives.

Harry S Truman, 33rd President of the U.S.

No one would have ever predicted that Harry Truman would become one of the greatest presidents in our history. He never attended college, and he failed in business, first as a farmer and later as part owner of a clothing store. He was over 50 when he was elected to his first national office.

But Truman was a fountain of knowledge and had rock-solid values shaped by years of reading. He read the Bible from cover to cover several times before he was 14 years old. He also read every volume of the *Encyclopaedia Britannica*, and all the novels of Charles Dickens and Victor Hugo, among others, as well as all the plays and sonnets of William Shakespeare.

> *Not every reader is a leader,*
> *but every leader must be a reader.*
>
> *—Harry Truman*

Truman's broad reading in the classics and his intimate knowledge of religion equipped him to lead America through the end of WWII and into the prosperous post-war period. He understood that reading was the cornerstone for a first-rate leader, and reading prepared Truman to make the tough decisions he faced, many of which were controversial and unpopular, such as the firing of the well-loved war hero, General Douglas MacArthur, for insubordination.

In his words, "Not every reader is a leader, but every leader must be a reader."

W. Clement Stone, Businessman

W. Clement Stone, founder of one of the largest insurance companies in the world, says his life was changed forever in 1937 when a salesman gave him a copy of *Think and Grow Rich*.

"When I read *Think and Grow Rich*," Stone says, "its philosophy coincided with my own in so many respects that I, too, started the habit of helping others by giving them inspirational self-help books."

Stone credits the book with transforming his business by teaching him the power of the mastermind principle—two or more people blending their individual talents to create wealth and solve problems.

"I did think—and grow rich," Stone says. "The mastermind principle made me realize that I could employ others to do much of the work I was doing, and thus, I would have more time for other activities."

Stone's story is proof that books are the best medium for the best thinkers in history to communicate their observations to the world. As George Will, the highly respected conservative columnist for *Newsweek* magazine, puts it, "I believe that the book still is the primary carrier of ideas."

Peter Drucker, Management Expert

At age 89, Peter Drucker is more active than most 25 year olds. He travels the world consulting with presidents of Fortune 500 companies like Sony, GM, and GE. He's continually working on a new book—to date he has published 29, most of which have become bestsellers. And he still finds time to read three to five hours a day on a wide range of subjects—a habit he first cultivated as a young man.

> *In our new knowledge economy, if you haven't learned how to learn, you'll have a hard time.*
> —Peter Drucker

"Every few years I pick another major topic and read in it daily for three years," Drucker says candidly. "It's not enough to make me an expert, but it's long enough to understand what the field is all about. I've been doing this for 60 years."

Some quick math tells you that Drucker has become very knowledgeable in 20 different fields, everything from economics to English literature to ancient Chinese history. Drucker is the epitome of the "knowledge worker," a term he coined to describe the most valuable resource in the new economy—intellectual capital.

"Your knowledge and your experience are your new wealth," explains Drucker. "They belong to you, not your company. Leave an organization and you take that wealth with you."

"In our new knowledge economy," Drucker continues, "if you haven't learned how to learn, you'll have a hard time. Knowing how to learn is partly curiosity. But it's also discipline." Drucker is living proof that the discipline of reading will be well rewarded in the Information Age.

Matthew McConaughey, Actor

The story of how a book changed Matthew McConaughey, the young Hollywood actor who had the leading role in John

Grisham's best-selling novel, *A Time to Kill*, is especially endearing to me because it was the same book that changed my life—*The Greatest Salesman in the World*.

"I was enrolled at the University of Texas with the idea of studying law," McConaughey says, "but I wasn't sleeping well with that idea. I read the first two chapters of *The Greatest Salesman in the World*, and I knew right then that I wanted to go to film school. I changed my major the next day."

While still in college, McConaughey was cast in a low-budget movie, *Dazed and Confused*. McConaughey was so good during the filming that the director expanded his part by writing new and longer scenes for his character. The result was a standout performance that got Hollywood's attention. Within months of moving to Los Angeles, he had landed major roles in big-budget films, including *A Time to Kill* and Stephen Spielberg's *Amistad*.

For sure, Matthew McConaughey has talent and good looks, but the same can be said for thousands of college-age students who have flirted with the notion of becoming an actor. The difference is McConaughey did something about it. Reading one book didn't dramatically increase his knowledge level, as was the case with the other people profiled above. But reading a book—one single, solitary book—did *increase his knowledge of himself*. Reading *The Greatest Salesman in the World* transformed Matthew McConaughey by making him aware of his true passion, and it helped him to understand that growing rich meant growing your God-given talents, not just growing your bank account.

> *Reading, like no other medium, can transform your life in a flash, and you never know which book... at which time in your life... might be the one that rocks your world and inspires you to grow in ways you never thought possible.*
>
> —Burke Hedges

You Never Know Which Book Will Change Your Life

Like Matthew McConaughey, I've been fortunate to grow both my talents and my bank account over the years. And, like McConaughey, a book was the catalyst that ignited my decision to make some changes in my life.

That's the beauty of reading: It has the power to make immediate transformations in your life through brilliant insights. And it has the power to make gradual transformations through accumulated knowledge. Either way, reading will expand your universe and grow you in ways you can never anticipate.

Reading is so powerful that a single book, or even a single sentence, for that matter, can change your life, like *The Greatest Salesman in the World* did for Matthew McConaughey and me. I doubt if he picked up the book with the idea of reading two chapters and then changing the direction of his career the next day. I know I didn't approach the book that way.

But again I say, the written word is so powerful it has the potential to stop you dead in your tracks and make you reverse the direction of your life. Reading, like no other medium, can transform your life in a flash, and you never know which book... at which time in your life... might be the one that rocks your world and inspires you to grow in ways you never thought possible before. *Amazing!*

3

The Slight Edge—
Reading 15 Minutes a Day
Can Change Your Life

Resolve to edge in a little reading every day,
if it is but a single sentence.
If you gain 15 minutes a day, it will make
itself felt at the end of the year.

—Horace Mann
American Educator

"WHEEL OF FORTUNE", HOSTED by Pat Sajak, is one of the most watched TV shows in the world. The game show is broadcast to 51 worldwide markets and reaches 100 million viewers each week.

Sajak has been hosting *Wheel of Fortune* for almost 20 years now, so it's safe to say he's an expert on the game. When an interviewer asked Sajak the key to winning big on the show, he made this observation:

I've never told anyone this. People who have a lot of money and not many letters up on the board... they don't know the puzzle and there are a lot of blank spaces... they're spinning that wheel and calling letters at random, instead of buying a vowel. I've seen more people lose a game without buying a vowel.

Reading Is Your Vowel

I've watched the show enough to know exactly what Pat Sajak is talking about. Sometimes there will just be a few letters up on the board and lots of blank spaces. Then one of the contestants will buy a vowel and Vanna White goes to work— flip... flip... flip.... Pretty soon I can start to make out a word or two. Before long the contestant has filled in so many letters that our family dog can solve the puzzle. The key to solving the puzzle can be traced to the *slight edge* the contestant got by buying a vowel.

> *It's not the most intellectual job in the world, but I do have to know the letters.*
>
> —Vanna White

I think the same thing happens in the game of life. People look at their lives and see a big puzzle with lots of blank spaces. So what do most people do? They start spinning their wheel of fortune and calling letters at random. "Try this... no, try this... let's buy that...."

Hello-o-o-o-o! It's time to quit calling letters at random, folks. It's time to get a slight edge in your life by buying a vowel... and one of the vowels in the game of life is reading. In short, *reading is your slight edge to help you solve the puzzles in your life.*

Now, when I talk about a "slight edge," I'm not talking about a monumental edge, like winning the lottery or inheriting a zillion dollars. I'm not talking a pie-in-the-sky edge. When I say a "slight edge," I'm talking about a small strategy that you can use again and again to give you a big advantage in the game of life. Let me give you a couple statistics that prove my point:

Statistic 1:
At any given time, one-third of Americans are living in poverty.

Statistic 2:
37% of Americans never read another book after high school.

Now think about those two statistics for a moment. America represents the greatest accumulation of wealth in the history of the world—and one out of three of us is living in poverty. That's a national disgrace! And more than one-third of us refuse to take advantage of the most powerful technological breakthrough in history—reading.

Let's see—one-third in poverty and one-third who don't read. Coincidence? I don't think so!

According to the National Center for Family Literacy, 40 million adults lack the reading skills to fill out a simple form. And 50 million aren't prepared for the high-tech jobs of the future. That's a total of 90 million adults in a population of 275 million people who cannot, or will not, use reading as a slight edge to improve their lives. That's almost one-third of the population who are "calling letters at random instead of buying a vowel" in the game of life. Without reading, they're setting themselves up to lose the game.

Reading may be a slight edge, folks, but it can yield such huge dividends! It's a shame millions of literate people lack the wisdom and the discipline to grow rich by reading 15 minutes or more a day.

Go Get the Information

Harvey Mackay, author of the bestselling book *Swim with the Sharks without Getting Eaten Alive!*, has this to say about the power of reading:

> *Our lives change in two ways: through the people we meet and the books we read.*

If you aren't meeting new people and reading new books, guess what—you're not changing. And if you're not changing, you're not growing. It's that simple.

Look, I realize that not every person who is happy and financially free is a reader... and not every reader is happy and financially free. That goes without saying. What I'm talking about is giving yourself a slight edge so that you're better today than you were yesterday. I'm talking about giving yourself a chance to win the game of life by buying a vowel! I'm talking about reading and growing rich in all areas of your life!

Having books in your home and not reading them in the Information Age would be like having seeds in your hand and not planting them in the Agricultural Age. In Denis Waitley's words, "The future belongs to those who learn what they need to learn in order to do what they need to do." In an age when "knowledge workers" vastly outnumber blue collar workers, you better be prepared to get the knowledge... and get it NOW!

A Few Overlooked Benefits of Reading

The other day I was talking to a publisher about the slight edge of reading, and I asked him point blank, "What is it about reading that sets it apart from any other way we get information?"

He thought for a moment before delivering a simple, yet profound, answer that immediately clarifies why reading remains the most powerful means of acquiring information ever invented.

"You can scan when you read," he said softly.

"That's it!" I thought. "That's why reading will never be replaced by TV... or movies... or conversation... or anything else humans are likely to invent. *You can scan when you read!* What an amazing advantage when you're looking for specific information in a limited period of time. You scan!

Ever try to scan an audio or video? It's a real pain. Every time I fast forward, I always end up missing the part I'm looking for. But it's so easy to scan when you're reading a book. Computer screens are harder to scan than books because you have to scroll, but programmers are sensitive to the problem and are doing a better job laying out text.

Take Notes While You Read

Another advantage of reading is that you can highlight key parts and write notes in the margins (try doing that on an audio tape!). Abraham Lincoln's law partner, Billy Herndon, remarked that Lincoln was a great one to underline text and write notes in margins of books. When Lincoln was especially intent on remembering parts of a book or document, he would underline entire pages and rewrite them in longhand.

This method may have been time consuming, but few could quibble with the results. As a lawyer in Springfield, Illinois, Lincoln argued scores of cases before the Illinois Supreme Court, and judges and opposing attorneys were always amazed at his thorough knowledge of the case at hand, as well as how he would masterfully illustrate his points by using stories he'd read from the Bible or Greek mythology.

Research and Cost

Can you remember the last time you researched a topic? Maybe you needed information on a new car you were considering buying. Or maybe you were planning a long-overdue vacation. A few years back you probably went to your local library or bookstore for help. That's how I used to do a lot of my research, too. Then, a couple years ago, someone showed me how to access the Internet. WOW! Suddenly I had the Information Age right at my fingertips!

Today I use the Internet as my primary research tool. If I want to find out what a new Mercedes costs, for example, I'll type in the word "Mercedes" in the search box of a web browser and... voila, within seconds I have tens of thousands of websites to choose from, everything from dealerships... to 'financing... to used parts... to auctions. With the Internet, I don't have to go to the library to do my research—*the library comes to me*!

Most amazing of all, this thing called the Internet is still in its infancy. One expert predicts that by the year 2003 there will be more than 10 million websites on the Internet. Information Age, I guess!

Just 10 years ago the worldwide web was available only to a few key people in the military. Private citizens couldn't gain access to the web at any cost. But today virtually anyone with a computer and a phone line can have instant access to the Internet for a few bucks a day—and the costs keep going down, down, down.

There was a time in this country when people could be excused for being illiterate. Or ignorant. That day is long gone. If someone truly wants to acquire information and knowledge, they can find it with just a little effort. People who can't afford the Internet at home still have access to thousands of public libraries across the country—and they're free!

Sales Are Up, but Reading Is Down

The book business is big business nowadays, that's for sure. Every year there are 60,000 new books published, and sales have been growing at a rate of 5% to 6% a year for the last decade.

That's the good news. The bad news is 50% of the books sold in this country are never read! Amazing, isn't it?... people buy books with the intention of reading and growing, but half the people don't follow through and read them. That's like paying money to join a health club and then never showing up. Du-h-h-h! We don't get the benefit when we buy a product. We get the benefit when we *use* the product! What are these people thinking about, anyway?

The truth is that every literate person in the world could enjoy the slight edge of reading if they would just take a little initiative. Having books and information readily available isn't enough. In order to grow rich, we have to READ the information and then apply it to our lives.

Cargo Cults of the South Pacific

The phenomenon of buying books and failing to read them reminds me of the "cargo cults" that still exist in several remote South Pacific islands. Some of these islands are populated by oral cultures that have had limited contact with the outside world. Until WWII, most of these islands were unexplored by people from industrialized countries. Even today the natives remain isolated from the outside world, except for occasional visits from foreign navies or emergency Red Cross workers.

> *The future belongs to those who learn what they need to learn in order to do what they need to do.*
>
> —Denis Waitley

During these rare visits from outsiders, the islanders would witness a magical phenomenon: When outsiders would scribble symbols on a piece of white paper and hand it to other outsiders, it meant the islanders would soon receive wonderful blessings from the gods. Giant "birds" would drop food and supplies from the sky. Giant boats would deliver crates of shoes, clothing, blankets, and tents.

The unsophisticated islanders mistakenly assumed that the commercial papers—proposals, purchase orders, invoices, and the like—were the *cause* of their good fortune and the *effect* was the shipment of supplies. The natives reasoned that if they performed the same actions as the outsiders, they could get the same results. So over the years they devised elaborate ceremonies, scribbling nonsense marks on paper and passing them along to cult members in the mistaken belief that their ritual would cause more cargo to magically appear.

People in literate cultures may smile at the innocence of the South Pacific islanders, yet all too many Americans do the same thing when they buy books they never read. Buying books *doesn't cause* people's lives to become magically enriched anymore than scribbling nonsense words on paper *causes* supplies to fall magically from the sky.

The fact is, buying books only makes you poorer. *Reading books is what makes you richer!*

"I Don't Have Time to Read"

Now, I realize that people buy books with the best of intentions. They honestly *intend* to read them when they pay the cashier. But let's face it, people are busier than ever today. Things come up. Life happens. And before they know it, it's bedtime and they're exhausted.

There's just no time to read.

Well, what if the government passed a law that would give $1 million cash to every American who would read 15 minutes every day without fail for one year? Do you think most people would suddenly *take* the time to read? Of course they would! They would rearrange their priorities to include reading because of the payoff, wouldn't they?

Now, notice I said they could *take* more time—not *make* more time—than they had before. We've all been given 24 hours a day. No more, no less. So we can't really *make* more time. But if people got paid cash to read, they'd rearrange their schedules to *take* the time to read, you can bet on that!

15 Minutes a Day = a Dozen Books a Year!

Okay... fantasy's over! The government's not going to make you financially richer by paying you to read. But you can definitely *grow richer* in your life by reading 15 minutes a day. In fact, you can read a book a month—that's 12 books a year—by reading only 15 minutes every day. Here's how:

The average high school graduate reads 250 words a minute. But we all stop to re-read a sentence from time to time... or pause to think about a new idea. So it's fair to say the average reading rate for most adults is 200 words per minute.

There are 400 or so words on this page, which means the average reader can easily read this page in two minutes. At that rate, you could read seven of these pages in a 15-minute period.

There are 132 pages in this book, including the introduction and conclusion. So by reading 15 minutes a day— that's seven pages—every day, you could read this book in 20 days, correct? It may take you more than a month to read some longer books, but by and large, if you'll read 15 minutes a day, you'll be able to finish a book a month.

By the end of the year, you'll have read at least 12 books, correct? By the end of 10 years, that will add up to 120 books! Just think, by setting aside just 15 minutes a day, you could easily read 120 books that could help you grow richer in all areas of your life. By doubling your daily reading time to just half an hour, you could read 25 books a year—that's 250 books in 10 years! Where else can you get that kind of return in less time than it takes to wash the dishes?

That's why I'm not too sympathetic with people who say they don't have time to read and grow rich. That's nonsense. They have the time. They're just choosing to use their time doing something they value more than reading. As I said, the slight edge can pay HUGE dividends, but only if we invest the time and discipline to read each and every day.

Think of Excuses TO Read

What about you?... Are you making excuses and justifying why you're settling for less than you deserve—like I used to do before I read *The Greatest Salesman in the World*? Are you too tired? Too busy? Too stressed out?

Well, instead of finding excuses NOT to read, why don't you find excuses TO read? Why not tell yourself you *deserve to grow richer* in all areas of your life? Why not tell yourself there's *no time like the present?*

Tell yourself that 15 minutes a day is only 1% of your entire day, and 1% of your time is a tiny, tiny investment compared to a HUGE payoff!

Tell yourself that you're going to use the slight edge of reading to get big dividends in your life.

Tell yourself to open one of those books you bought a while back but haven't started yet... and then tell yourself to read for 15 minutes.

After you close your book for the day, tell yourself how much richer you are for reading.

Oh, and tell yourself that you're not going to lose the game of life because you didn't stop and buy a vowel.

Tell yourself you're smarter than that.

Because you are.

4

How to Read a Book

*There is a great deal of difference between
the eager man who wants to read a book and
the tired man who wants a book to read.*
                                    —G.K. Chesterton

HOW'S THIS FOR IRONY?... you read three chapters in
this book and then come across a chapter telling you how to
read a book!

Huh-h-h?!! What's the author think I've been doing—
knitting?

I suppose I should have called this chapter, "How to Read
a Book *Effectively*," because there's a big difference between
reading a book and *understanding the message in the book*. That's
what this chapter will teach you—how to read a book so that
you not only get the information but understand the message
more fully.

Reading Is Like Playing Golf

The best way to explain what I mean by *effective reading* is to
compare reading to another passion in my life—golf. I'll be

the first to admit that golf is an easy game to love, but a tough game to master. I belong to three country clubs, and I bet I can count on one hand the number of golfers who consistently shoot par.

> *Reading furnishes the mind only with materials of knowledge; it is thinking that makes what we read ours.*
>
> —John Locke

One thing all the best players have in common is that they took the time to learn the fundamentals, and then they practice those fundamentals over and over again. Like I always say, "Practice doesn't make perfect. Only *perfect practice* makes perfect." That's why there are a lot more hackers than scratch golfers—the hackers never took the time to learn the fundamentals, so when they practice, they're reinforcing their bad habits.

I'm amazed at the number of guys who brag that they've never had a lesson. "I'm self-taught," they say. Then they go out and spray the ball all over the course, all the while complaining that "today is just not my day." No, and tomorrow won't be their day, either, as long as they lack the fundamentals.

My point is that 99% of the golfers could dramatically improve their games by taking six to 10 lessons from a club pro and then religiously practicing what they have learned. If every hacker had the wisdom to first learn and practice how to *play golf effectively*, they would get much better results, wouldn't you agree?

The same can be said for reading a book. Research shows that readers who have the wisdom to *learn how to read a book effectively* get much better results; that is, they understand the material better and remember it much longer.

Three-Step Reading System

Before I get started, let me draw an analogy that will better explain the roles of the writer and the reader. I first came across this analogy in the classic best-seller, *How to Read a Book*, by Mortimer Adler and Charles Van Doren, first published in 1940.

Think of the writer as the pitcher and the reader as the catcher. The catcher's job is just as active as the pitcher's, although the activities are very different. As the catcher gets more active and more skilled, he becomes better at catching all kinds of pitches—fastballs... curveballs... changeups... knuckle-balls... foul balls... even wild pitches. "Similarly," Adler and Van Doren write, "the art of reading is the skill of catching every sort of communication as well as possible."

> *I took a course in speed reading and was able to read "War and Peace" in 20 minutes.*
> *It's about Russia.*
> —Woody Allen

What follows are three steps that are guaranteed to help you improve your skill as a "catcher of written messages." By following these steps, you will increase the depth of your understanding when you read, thereby becoming a more effective reader. The three steps are as follows.

1) pre-read the book
2) read actively and take notes
3) review your notes

In the next few pages we'll take a brief look at each step.

Step 1: Pre-Read the Book

Let me ask you a question. If you were shopping for a house, would you buy an existing home based on a bunch of photographs, even if you loved what you saw? I sure hope not.

Before you'd commit to buying the home, you'd want to visit the neighborhood. Walk around the house, inside and out. Measure the rooms and peek in the closets. Check out the local schools. Take a drive to the nearest shopping mall. Talk to neighbors. Compare the price of the house to similar ones in the neighborhood. Check out how long it takes to commute to work. Stuff like that.

In other words, if you liked what you saw in the photographs, you'd want to see how the house fit into the big picture, wouldn't you? Well, the same goes for reading a book. Before diving right in and starting to read, you need to take a few minutes to "see the big picture" of a book. This is what is known as "pre-reading" the book.

Here are some tips that will help you get an overview of a new book. First thing you need to do is read the front and back cover. Read the testimonials or the summary statement on the back cover. Read the author's biography so you understand how his credentials relate to the topic at hand.

> *Anyone who can read can learn how to read deeply and thus live more fully.*
>
> —*Norman Cousins*

Open the book to the introductory pages and skim them. Has the author written other books on the subject? Who is the book dedicated to? Any special acknowledgments? Read the foreword, preface, and introduction. Many readers skip these sections, thinking they're a waste of time. But they can give you valuable insights into the book's main points.

Take a few minutes to skim the table of contents. The contents page will give you a blueprint of the book and let you know how the author has chosen to unfold his arguments. The great American author Ernest Hemingway once remarked that good writing is architecture, not interior design. So analyze the architecture of a book before you begin reading. After reviewing the table of contents, turn to the beginning of each chapter and read the chapter titles and skim the opening paragraph. If the chapter has subtitles or headlines, thumb through the chapters and read the headlines. These will provide you with an outline of each chapter.

Pre-Reading Can Make a World of Difference

Now, this whole process of "pre-reading" might seem a bit unnecessary, given the fact you are going to read the book anyway. But pre-reading can make the difference between understanding an author's message and totally missing the point. Here's a true-life story that serves to illustrate the ¬ucial importance of pre-reading:

World-famous psychologist B.F. Skinner was a leading exponent of behaviorism, a school of psychology based on the belief that free will is an illusion, for all human behavior can be predicted by positive or negative reinforcement. When Skinner was introduced to George Bernard Shaw, the great Irish dramatist and social critic, the psychologist thanked Shaw for writing the book that changed his life.

"Your book inspired my career," gushed Skinner. "It convinced me once and for all of the profound truth behind behaviorism."

"You must be kidding!" replied a stunned Shaw. "I thought my book destroyed the argument of behaviorism once and for all!"

As the two men talked, it soon became clear why Skinner received a different message from Shaw's book. Shaw had saved his final argument against behaviorism for the last chapter, but Skinner had never finished the book. Because he hadn't read the last chapter, he had totally misinterpreted the main message of the book!

> *The art of reading is the skill of catching every sort of communication as well as possible.*
>
> —Mortimer Adler & Charles Van Doren

If Skinner had pre-read the book, he would have noticed that Shaw had intentionally built a case for behaviorism in the early chapters in order to tear it down in the last one. But an incomplete reading by Skinner gave him an entirely different perspective and influenced him in ways the author never intended.

Pre-reading may add an extra 10 minutes to the reading of a book, but it is time well spent, for it can dramatically increase comprehension and understanding.

Step 2: Read Actively

Do you remember our definition of reading from an earlier chapter? *Reading is visually guided thinking.* Keep that definition in mind as we discuss *Step 2: Read Actively*, because active reading and "visually guided thinking" are really one and the same.

Active reading is nothing more than the mental process of asking and answering questions in order to gather information and increase our understanding. It stands to reason that readers who ask more and better questions—that is, deeper, more probing questions—will be rewarded with a richer reading experience. In other words, the more active we become as readers, the richer our reward.

Ask the Tough Questions—and Lots of Them!

In order to read and grow rich, we have to start asking more questions, and the kinds of questions we ask become more probing. That's what the expression "read between the lines" is all about. When we read between the lines, we don't take the written information at face value. We look deeper. We think harder. We ask tougher questions. We try to get to the *real* meaning. We're trying to increase our understanding of the text and, in so doing, increase our understanding of ourselves and our world.

> *Good writing is architecture, not interior design.*
> —*Ernest Hemingway*

To best explain the difference between reading superficially for information and reading actively for understanding, take a look at *Alice's Adventures in Wonderland* by Lewis Carroll. When children read the book, they are mostly seeking to read for information, and they find the plot and the strange characters in the book delightful and entertaining.

But Carroll's classic children's story can be read at a much deeper level, as evidenced by the fact that *Alice's Adventures in Wonderland* is the third-most quoted book in the English language, after the Bible and Shakespeare's plays and sonnets. When adults read *Alice's Adventures in Wonderland* for understanding, they are treated to a major work of literature with many layers of meaning.

Francis Bacon wrote that "some books are to be tasted... others to be swallowed... and more few to be chewed and digested." When we read for understanding, we're chewing and digesting the text.

Take Notes

Asking and answering questions while reading is the primary way readers go about making a book their own.

I take the ownership concept of a book literally, which is why I prefer to buy books rather than check them out from the library. When I read I like to have a highlighter and a pen with me, and I mark key passages and write notes in the margins as I go along.

Over the years I've come up with my own system of note-taking during reading. I underline or circle key concepts. I put big stars by key passages. I highlight quotes that I might use for future books and speeches. And I write down the page numbers containing the key themes on the back inside cover for future reference.

As you make notes in your own books, you'll develop your own system. Not only will note-taking help you internalize the material, but it will make it a lot easier to locate key passages in the future.

Step 3 : Review Your Notes

The final stage of the three-step reading system to increase understanding is the review stage. After you complete a book, congratulate yourself for seeing the task through to the end, and then set it aside. A week or so later, pick the book back up and give it a quick 10-minute review.

This is when the note-taking comes in handy. As you thumb through the book, read your notes and the highlighted material again. Take a few moments to think about the questions and comments you wrote. As you review, you'll be amazed at how fresh and new the material seems, even though you just finished the book a few days ago. You'll also be amazed to discover that your comments were well thought out and that you did a good job of highlighting most of the key themes, statistics, and arguments.

> *Some books are to be tasted... others to be swallowed... and more few to be chewed and digested.*
>
> —Francis Bacon

The best way to explain the value of reviewing is to tell you the joke about the little girl and the watermelon.

A little girl visited a farm one day and asked to buy a large watermelon.

"That big one you got your hand on costs three dollars," the farmer said.

"I've only got 30 cents," replied the little girl.

"Thirty cents will only buy you a small watermelon," replied the farmer. "How about that one?" he said, pointing to a small watermelon in the field.

"*Okay, I'll take it,*" smiled the little girl. "*Here's your 30 cents. But leave it on the vine. I'll be back for it in a month.*"

Pretty smart little girl, isn't she? She knew that her patience would be rewarded. By waiting one month, she could have a big, ripe watermelon for the price of a little green one.

Read Now, Reap Later

Like the little girl, we're rewarded in a big way when we review books weeks—or even months and years—after we first read them. We're amazed at how much we've forgotten as we review a book, and the insights and understanding come flooding back as we skim the highlighted sections, reminding us that the review was well worth the wait.

Reviewing a book will also remind you that there is a big return on the time and effort you spent in reading. Like the stock market, sometimes we don't recognize that return until much later—even years later.

But the return on reading is very big... and very real... as you will learn in the next chapter, called, *The Readers and the Read-Nots vs. The Haves and the Have-Nots*.

5

The Readers & the Read-Nots vs. The Haves & the Have-Nots

*Reading is cumulative and proceeds
by geometrical progression:
each new reading builds upon
whatever the reader has read before.*

—Alberto Manguel
from *A History of Reading*

I OFTEN TELL THE STORY about the two boys who were out walking in the woods when they looked up to see a huge grizzly bear charging in their direction.

The boys took off running as fast as they could. Suddenly, one of the boys stopped, pulled his tennis shoes out of his backpack, and started lacing them up as fast as he could.

"What are you doing?!!!" screamed his friend. "Those tennis shoes won't help you outrun a bear!"

"I don't need to outrun the bear," the other boy shouted as he sprinted away in his tennis shoes. *"I only need to outrun you!"*

Parable of the Haves and the Have-Nots
This story serves as a parable for the race between the "haves" and the "have-nots," a phenomenon that is occurring with

ever-increasing frequency as the Information Age gains momentum.

Think of the charging grizzly as increasing competition and the two boys as workers in the Information Age. The tennis shoes are what I call the "slight edge of reading"; that is, a seemingly small but crucial advantage that will spell the difference between survival and disaster.

> *The man who does not read good books has no advantage over the man who can't read them.*
>
> —Mark Twain

The boy with the tennis shoes—the reader— will not only survive in the Information Age, he will thrive, for he has prepared himself for the challenges ahead. *The reader will go on to become one of the haves.*

The boy without the tennis shoes, however, will become a victim of the hard-charging Information Age. *The read-not will become one of the have-nots.*

The Growing Income Gap

The gap between the haves and the have-nots is real and it's getting wider by the day. Twenty years ago, it took a CEO one week to earn what the average worker earned in a year. Today it takes that same CEO *one day* to earn what the average worker earns in a year. Folks, that's not a wage gap—that's a *wage gulf*—and it's occurring across all job levels.

Take a look at these average earning figures from a 1995 U.S. Census Bureau survey:

Education Level	Average Annual Income
Didn't complete high school	$ 11,000
High school graduate	$ 17,000
College graduate	$ 32,000
Master's degree	$ 41,000
Attorneys and doctors	$ 66,000

What does this chart tell us? Well, the figures tell us that an investment in education pays big dividends, that's for sure. But I'm more interested in what the chart *doesn't* tell us. Let me explain.

Look at the figures on the right again. They represent *average annual incomes.* They aren't chiseled in stone. Not every person who graduates from college is automatically entitled to earn $32,000 a year. I personally know several college grads who are earning minimum wage, and I know some high school dropouts who earn far more than the average professional.

Why is it that some people do better than the average, while others do worse? Well, it's my contention that the workers who take advantage of reading will outperform non-readers virtually every time. That's why I always tell people that the best edge in the new economy is still the old technology—reading!

And I don't just mean an edge in earning power, either. Reading gives you an edge to make you richer in relationships... happiness... fulfillment... contentment... career satisfaction... and so on.

> *Those who can read see twice as well.*
> —Meander

This chart is a testimony to Ben Franklin's sage observation that "an investment in knowledge pays the best interest." When Franklin made that observation, America was in the midst of the Agricultural Age, a period in history when 90% of the people in this country lived and worked on farms.

Today we're in the midst of the Information Age, a period in history when fewer than 2% of the population live on farms. Knowledge is 1,000 times more important today than it was during Franklin's lifetime. And reading is still the best way to get the knowledge so that you can ride the crest of the Information Age wave, rather than drown in its wake.

80/20 Rule Applies to Reading

We've all heard the 80/20 rule—20% of the workers in any given occupation do 80% of the work. Here's the way the 80/20 rule applies to adult-age Americans:

> 20% are illiterate or read poorly; they read seldom, if ever
> 60% can read reasonably well but are choosing not to read
> 20% can read well and are reading frequently

Let's start our discussion of the 80/20 rule with the 20% who read poorly or are illiterate. You'll soon see the accuracy of the opening parable, for there's an overwhelming correlation between not-reading and not-having —and the outlook for non-readers isn't pretty.

Illiteracy: Running in Quicksand

There was a time not too long ago when poor readers could make a pretty good living for themselves and their families. Assembly line workers at Ford or Caterpillar or Goodyear could punch the clock and put in the time, boring as it was, and support a family of four in pretty good style. They owned their own homes and drove decent cars. Some even managed to send their kids to college.

Every man who knows how to read has it in his power to magnify himself, to multiply the ways in which he exists, to make his life full, significant, and interesting.

—Aldous Huxley

But as the Industrial Age continues to give way to the Information Age, there are fewer and fewer high-paying factory jobs available. For people lacking in skills and knowledge today, the job prospects are thin—and getting thinner.

As a result, there are a lot of angry, frustrated people out there. No matter how hard these people work, they just keep getting further and further behind. It's like the bumper sticker I saw recently. It said: "The faster I runs, the behinder I gets!" Poor readers must feel like they're trying to run in quicksand—the more they struggle, the deeper they sink in anger and frustration.

Angry at the World

There's a whole bunch of people who can't live their dreams because they can't read. The National Institute for Literacy reports that more than 20% of adults read at or below the fifth grade level—that's 40 million Americans over the age of 16! Plus, 43% of people with the lowest literacy levels live in poverty. Welfare recipients ages 17 to 21 read, on average, at the sixth grade level. How do you think *they feel?* How would *you feel* in their shoes? I know I'd be angry—*really angry!*

Our prisons are filled with poor readers and illiterates who chose to express their anger at the world by hurting themselves through drug abuse... or worse, by hurting others through stealing or random acts of violence. Here are some sobering statistics from the Correctional Education Association to prove my point:

- Only 51% of prisoners have completed high school, compared to 75% of the general population
- 70% of prisoners scored in the bottom two literacy levels
- An Illinois study found that 62% of the released inmates with an eighth grade education or less were re-arrested

When I look at these statistics, I'm reminded of a wise, old saying: "If your only tool is a hammer, every problem looks like a nail." People who can't read have fewer tools than readers, and, as a result, they are more likely to bludgeon their way through life.

Sadly, this is no small number of Americans. The National Center for Family Literacy estimates that one in 10 high school graduates can't read well enough to fill out a job application!

Some students drink at the fountain of knowledge. Others just gargle.

—E. C. McKenzie

The good news is there are scores of programs available for adults who want to become better readers. The National Center's programs are helping 60,000 families to read, and their programs are working wonders! Studies show that the need for public assistance drops 50% for families who graduate from the center's programs!

Can Read, but Don't

Now let's look at the big bulge on the bell curve—the 60% who can read but are choosing NOT to. These are the people who have the greatest tool for self-improvement available to them, but, for one reason or another, are choosing NOT to use it.

Here's a scary statistic: More than 37% of all high school graduates never read a book after high school. What are these people doing with their time? Two letters tell the story—TV.

A recent book called *Time for Life* by John Robinson and Geoffrey Godbey, says the average American has 37 hours of free time per week—five hours more than 30 years ago. So how are they choosing to spend it? By watching more TV! TV now takes up a stupefying 40% of the average American's free time.

> *An investment in knowledge pays the best interest.*
>
> —Ben Franklin

"TV is clearly the 800-pound gorilla of free time," the authors write. "We have encountered people who tell us they don't have any free time *because* they are watching TV." Amazing! Some people consider TV a necessity instead of an option!

The U.S. Census Bureau reveals that the average person spent 1,595 hours watching TV in 1997, or just under 4.4 hours per day. Here's how most people spend their daily leisure time:

4.4 hours watching TV
3 hours listening to the radio
45 minutes listening to recorded music
27 minutes a day reading a newspaper
17 minutes a day reading books
14 minutes a day reading magazines.

In other words, the average American is spending over four hours watching TV and less than one hour reading! What do you think would happen if that figure were reversed? *Read and grow rich, I guess!*

Not Knocking TV

Please understand—I'm not knocking TV. Hey, our house has three TV sets, and one of them is a giant-screen model. In all honesty, I think TV is getting better all the time. Today there are hundreds of channels to choose from, and there's an increasing number of great educational channels to choose from, such as the History Channel or the Discovery Channel, to name just two.

But all too many people are wasting precious free time watching worthless fluff, or worse, watching glitzy programs that carelessly promote sex and violence. Too many Americans are like the little boy who tried to eat all of his birthday cake at one sitting—they're trying to watch everything on TV rather than choosing to exercise some discipline.

The authors of *Time for Life* sum up the situation this way: "Free time requires commitment, imagination, reflection, and discipline if we are to use it wisely."

Commitment, imagination, reflection, and discipline—hm-m-m, sounds to me like this is exactly what we do when we read!

Remember—Everything Counts!

All this talk about watching too much junk TV reminds me of the joke about a new diet. You eat whatever you want... whenever you want... and as much as you want. You don't lose any weight, but the diet's real easy to stick with!

The same can be said for our spare time. We can fill up our non-working hours with non-productive activities, and that's one "diet" that's certainly easy to stick to. But it won't help us get what we really want out of life, will it?

Don Shula, the Hall-of-Fame coach of the Miami Dolphins, used to tell his players that they were either getting better, or they were getting worse. There was no middle ground.

> *A competitive world has two possibilities. You can lose. Or, if you want to win, you can change.*
> —*Lester C. Thurow*

"So work hard and get better!" Shula urged his players.

The same goes for your life. You're either getting richer... or you're getting poorer—and I don't mean just in money. There is no middle ground. If you aren't using your leisure time to read and grow rich, guess what—you're heading in the other direction! World-renowned economist Lester C. Thurow puts it this way:

"A competitive world has two possibilities. You can lose.

Or, if you want to win, you can change."

I challenge all Americans who *can* read but are *choosing not to read* to change! No one in this country has to lose. We can all win! But if people are serious about becoming one of the haves, they must change their leisure-time habits.

I'm not suggesting people throw out their TVs. Just don't turn them on quite as often. And then read.

Like my friend Gary Blair says, *everything counts*!

The "haves" are making their spare time count. They're reading.

What about *you*?

6

Everyone—including *YOU*— Can Read & Grow Rich!

Books have meant to my life what the sun has meant to the planet Earth.

—Earl Nightingale

LATE ONE AFTERNOON Carol got the telephone call that every loving spouse dreads: *"This is Officer Williams of the Clearwater Police Department. Your husband was in a serious automobile accident. He's been taken by ambulance to Bayfront Community Hospital."*

Carol rushed to the hospital only to be greeted by a grim-faced doctor.

"I'm sorry," the doctor said. "We tried to save him but it was too late. I'm so sorry...."

A little background before I tell you how Carol handled this crisis. When Carol and Bill were first married, they had agreed that he'd be the breadwinner while she stayed at home with the kids. She hadn't worked out of the home since she was in her 20s. So, at 46 years old, Carol was forced to go back to work while raising two teen-agers by herself.

Carol set about rebuilding her shattered life. In truth, she didn't have much of a choice—it was sink or swim. She enrolled in a one-year program to become a paralegal. She talked endlessly to her friends and her minister. And she visited the library and bookstores, seeking books that would help her manage the flood of negative emotions she was experiencing—grief... anger... fear of failure... stress... worry... and depression.

Reading and Recovery

A life-long reader, Carol instinctively turned to books for comfort and guidance. Let's take a brief look at a few of the books Carol read to help her rebuild her life:

Tough Times Don't Last But Tough People Do—This book helped Carol accept the fact that we all must face harsh realities in this life, and it encouraged her to concentrate on her many blessings and to live in the present, not the past.

> *You are the same today as you'll be in five years except for two things, the people you meet and the books you read.*
>
> —Charles E. "T" Jones

Panic Attacks: What They Are and What to Do About Them—This book gave Carol an understanding of her frequent panic attacks and suggested coping strategies when she was feeling overwhelmed with fear and anxiety.

Stress Survival and Stress Management Handbook—These two books provided insights into dealing with stresses that Carol had never experienced before.

Making Change: A Woman's Guide to Designing Her Financial Future—For 20 years Bill made the money and paid the bills. This book gave Carol knowledge and confidence. Before the accident she couldn't even reconcile her checkbook. Today she's in charge of investing her retirement savings.

Reviving Ophelia—New challenges and conflicts arose as Carol's daughter entered her teen-age years. This book gave Carol insights into the fragile self-esteem of teen-age girls and made her aware of the emotional and physical changes her daughter would be going through.

The English Patient—This lyrical novel was turned into an Academy-Award-winning movie. The book reminded Carol that great literature, more than any other medium, can transport us through time by stimulating our imaginations and connecting with our emotions.

Memoirs of a Geisha—This beautifully written bestseller introduced Carol to a time in Japan's history when women were treated as objects of entertainment for powerful men, reminding her that things could be worse—a lot worse!

Angela's Ashes—The touching story of a boy growing up in abject poverty in Limerick, Ireland, the book is an excursion into our worst childhood fears and reminded Carol that love and a sense of humor can light even the darkest hours.

History of Art—A survey of history's greatest works of art, this book ignited Carol's spirits and rekindled her appreciation for beauty.

I'm telling you about these books because it illustrates how a person can use reading to deal with pain and change. Please understand that I'm not necessarily endorsing these books. Frankly, I haven't read a single page from any of them. But Carol will be the first to tell you that each of these books helped her grow rich in hope, spirit, optimism, and knowledge during the lowest point in her life.

We All Have Problems

Carol, of course, isn't the only person in this world with problems. The couple next door to her might have a happy marriage, but they might be three months behind on their mortgage payments. The couple next door to them might have lots of money and a good marriage, but they might be wrestling with how to handle their oldest son, who has a drug and alcohol problem. And so on, right on down the block... around the neighborhood... across the country... and around the world.

If you've got a pulse, you've got problems. That's what life is all about—recognizing and solving problems. I get the feeling that some people think that rich people have fewer problems than the rest of us—that all their problems would disappear if they only had money.

"If I had his money," you hear people say, "I wouldn't have a care in the world." Not true. Everybody has problems. You think Bill Gates, multi-billionaire president of Microsoft, doesn't have problems? As I write this, the government is coming down on his company with both feet, accusing him of conspiring to create a monopoly. He's got problems, all right— big problems! Guess what—once this problem is behind him, there will be a bunch more to take its place. He's the richest man in the world, and he's still got a lot of problems. There's just no escaping them!

That's why I say growing rich is more than growing your bank account. Growing rich in the fullest sense of the word is recognizing your problems and then solving them. Growing rich means growing into a better person.

Employ your time in improving yourself by other people's writings so you shall come easily by what others have labored hard for.

—*Socrates*

A recent Ziggy cartoon in the local paper offers these words of wisdom about problems: "*Don't measure yourself by the problems you face... measure yourself by the problems you've faced up to!!*" Both Carol and I are proof that books not only help us face our problems, but they also give us the wisdom and understanding to solve them, and, in the solving, we grow richer.

Reading & Growing Rich Is for Everyone!

In the rest of this chapter I'm going to tell you about people who, like Carol, have read and grown rich in their lives. The people you're about to meet come from all backgrounds and represent all levels of society, from prisoners to presidents. But the one thing they all have in common is they all grew richer from reading, proving that reading can transform everyone—even YOU—whether you are a government worker or a governor... a small business owner or a Fortune 500 CEO... a clerk or a middle manager... a homemaker or a breadwinner—you name it. Whoever you are or whatever you do, the hidden powers of reading can make you richer in all areas of your life.

Let's start our discussion with some people you'd least likely expect to grow rich from reading—inmates at a prison in Lincoln, Illinois.

Bedtime Stories from Prison

Like millions of mothers across the world, Erika Gonzales is reading a bedtime story to her two-year-old boy, Jimmy. The difference is she's reading into a cold, black tape recorder. Jimmy lives with Erika's sister 125 miles away. His 18-year-old mother lives in prison, serving a year for robbery and battery.

> *Read in order to live.*
>
> —Gustave Flaubert

"Mommy misses you and loves you," she speaks into the recorder. "I'm going to read you a book to let you know this is me and I love you." She finishes the story and hands the book and recorder to volunteers of the Storybook Project, who will mail the book and the tape to Jimmy.

The Storybook Project is built around a simple concept: Children need bedtime stories, even if their parents are in prison, and reading bedtime stories is just as valuable to the parents as it is to the kids.

Volunteers collect books and recorders, take them to prisons, and encourage inmates, both male and female, to record stories and personal messages for their children. The volunteers set up one of the prison classrooms, filling it with books. Inmates page through the books during their free time.

Some prisoners select several books that will appeal to all of their children. Others seek out religious books or books that teach moral lessons, such as how to share. Books for little children, like *Big Bird's Busy Day*, can be read in a matter of minutes. Books for older children take longer to read, so prisoners usually read the first chapter and encourage their children to finish the book for themselves.

Small Steps Add Up to Big Results

Inmates at the medium-security Logan Correctional Center

in central Illinois jumped at the chance to take part in the Storybook Project. Dozens of inmates signed up and every day more inmates are requesting permission to reach out and touch their children through reading.

"This program is not going to cure all of the family's problems," says one volunteer. "But I can't help thinking [that] from a child's perspective, it will be a memory of a loving moment."

I've got to believe it can be much more than that—it can be a powerful tool to help break the cycle of poverty and crime that is all too common in non-reading families. As Abigail Van Buren, better known as Dear Abby to her faithful readers, says:

Richer than I you will never be,
For I had a mother who read to me.

Rolling Readers Reaches Needy Kids

The Rolling Readers, California's largest nonprofit children's literacy organization, is similar to the Storybook Program in that its mission is to encourage reading among disadvantaged children. It was started in 1961 by a father who volunteered to read to kids at a homeless shelter after he noticed the profound effect reading had on his own children.

> *It is from books that wise men derive consolation in the troubles of life.*
> —*Victor Hugo*

Volunteers go to schools and shelters once a week and read aloud to classes. Three times a year they sponsor a book giveaway, when children get their own new books. Children love to hear volunteers read them stories, but they are thrilled to own their own books.

The Storybook Program and Rolling Readers may be small steps for people with big problems, but at least they're steps in the right direction. And never let us forget that small steps over time can add up to a journey that can take people far away from their underprivileged backgrounds.

Books Behind Bars

Reading can help troubled adults change their lives, too, as evidenced by a court-ordered reading program in Lowell, Massachusetts. Dozens of convicted criminals are doing time around a conference table instead of behind bars as part of a special program called Changing Lives Through Literature.

This isn't just another liberal version of "Let's get soft on criminals." The Changing Lives Through Literature program gets results! A survey of the 68 convicts who completed the classes showed that crime of all types among the graduates fell by 68%, while serious crime dropped 80%. Here's how the program works:

Instead of serving a jail sentence, the convicts enter a probationary period in which they enroll in the three-month course. The program is only available to convicts and repeat offenders who demonstrate a desire to change their lives. No sex offenders or murderers are allowed.

> *Don't measure yourself by the problems you face... measure yourself by the problems you've faced up to!!*
>
> —*Ziggy cartoon*

Participants read six novels, one book every two weeks. Here's a sample of the novels the Changing Lives Through Literature program uses to empower male convicts to read and grow rich: *The Old Man and the Sea*, by Ernest Hemingway; *Sea Wolf*, by Jack London; *Of Mice and Men*, by John Steinbeck; and *Deliverance*, by James Dickey.

If offenders cut class and don't have a viable excuse, they're sent to jail to serve their full sentences. An English professor, a judge, two probation officers, and a group of convicts meet every other week in a classroom setting. They all participate as equals, and the discussions center around values-driven topics, such as lessons on personal responsibility, self respect, and compassion.

"There's something magical that happens around that conference table," says Robert Waxler, a literature professor who started the experiment at the Dartmouth campus of the University of Massachusetts. "It's a discussion that allows everyone involved to be reflective about the characters in the stories—and about themselves."

Books Can Build a Better You

I truly believe in the power of books to build a better person, even if that person is a prison inmate. Not long ago I was invited to speak to inmates at a federal penitentiary in Florida. After my talk I handed out copies of my book, *You, Inc: Discover the CEO Within*. I still get letters from inmates telling me how the book has inspired them to rethink their lives. That's the beauty of books—they challenge us to think about our belief systems in new and different ways.

Remember the definition of reading from the first chapter?—*reading is visually stimulated thinking*. This definition best describes the reason that everyone from inmates to judges can benefit from reading, especially if experienced people guide the discussions. When people are encouraged to think about themselves and how they fit in with the rest of the world, they are forced to think about some inconsistencies in their lives. Re-evaluating our lives by thinking about our values is the first step to personal growth.

Spiritual Growth

There are so many ways that reading can help us grow—financially... emotionally... professionally... and, of course, spiritually. This next story concerns Earl Flowers, a minister in Los Angeles whose daily prayer was to grow richer in God's word by reading the Bible.

True, that doesn't seem like such a remarkable request for a minister. But Earl was different from most ministers. You see, until he was well into his 40s, he couldn't read. He knew the alphabet, and he could fake his way through a fourth grade illustrated book. But job applications, simple directions for assembling toys, or bedtime stories for his grandchildren were beyond his comprehension.

Earl was born in the Central American country of Belize, where he was abandoned as a young child. He lived for a while in a horse barn with nothing but the clothes on his back. But he was bright and ambitious, and he built several successful businesses in Belize before emigrating to the U.S.

He became a born-again Christian and founded the New Directions Christian Center in Los Angeles, relying on his great memory and skillful maneuvering to lead his congregation without ever actually reading from the pulpit. But by remain-

ing illiterate, he was denying himself one of the greatest plea-
sures in his life—reading and studying scripture.

Time to Change

I always tell people that when it gets harder to suffer than
change, you will change. One day Earl got tired of suffering
the indignity of illiteracy, and he walked into the Los Angeles
Public Library and asked for help. He was paired up with a
volunteer for the Library Adult Reading Project (LARP).

Earl and the volunteer met twice a week for several months,
working hard to master the literacy skills most people take for
granted, such as mastering the silent e and identifying root
words.

One day Earl opened his black briefcase and handed his
tutor two tickets to his church's annual celebration banquet.
Earl had been chosen to read the church's mission statement,
and he wanted the tutor to help him prepare for the event.
One big problem—the language in
the mission statement was formal
and advanced far beyond the
fourth grade, and the banquet was
in two weeks!

Earl read the statement while
the tutor identified the areas that
needed special attention. On
Earl's first read through, the tutor

> *Richer than I*
> *you will never be,*
> *for I had a mother*
> *who read to me.*
>
> —Abigail Van Buren

noted more than 40 words and phrases that Earl couldn't read.
The tutor had serious doubts that Earl could pull this off on
such short notice. But Earl was determined.

On the night of the banquet, when it was Earl's turn to
read, his wife leaned over and whispered to him, "Are you sure
you want to do this? I can read it for you."

"I can do this," Earl said. "Praise God, I can do this."

And read it he did. Every word. Without a single stutter.

To the assembled crowd, it sounded just like just another
man reading just another speech. But not to Earl Flowers and
his wife. To them it sounded like a miracle.

Not long after the reading, Earl showed up at the library
to tell his tutor some more great news—he had passed his test

to become an American citizen.

"I've been here for all these years and couldn't take the test 'cause I couldn't read," Earl explained. "It's funny, 'cause actually the test was easy! I scored 24 out of 25!"

God Helps Those Who Help Themselves

I love this story because Earl Flowers wasn't afraid to put it all on the line. He understood that he would never realize his full potential as a practicing Christian, much less a minister, unless he learned to read. So he faced up to his shortcomings and did what he had to do to remedy the situation. The Earl Flowers' of the world are living proof of the axiom "God helps those who help themselves."

Do you have any doubt in your mind that Earl is reading the Bible and growing richer for it, every single day of his life? I sure don't. In my mind, Earl is a true hero. He quit accommodating his limitations, choosing to conquer them instead. If that's not the definition of growing rich, I don't know what is!

If you asked Earl Flowers if it's really possible for everyone to read and grow rich, what do you think he'd say?

I'll bet he'd answer by reading you a passage from the Bible.

Reading Is the Best Revenge

So far we've talked about how reading can help people outside the mainstream—people like Earl Flowers, a functionally illiterate immigrant from Central America—grow richer in their lives.

Now let's look at how reading helped another outsider and his family grow richer. But this story has a twist. This outsider not only grew richer personally and professionally, but his contributions have enriched the lives of millions of people throughout the world!

The man's name is Michael DeBakey, and his life is evidence that reading has the power to elevate us to our highest levels of achievement. Here's his remarkable story:

DeBakey's parents emigrated from Lebanon to America as children, settling in Louisiana because French was their second language. The mother and father never had the opportunity to go to college, but they valued reading above all else, and they passed on their love of reading to their children. Michael DeBakey recalls how as a child he, his brother, and his two sisters were "required to go to the library each week, borrow a new book, and read it."

One week he came home depressed because the librarian wouldn't let him check out what he thought was the best book in the library. The "book" was the *Encyclopaedia Britannica*. DeBakey's father bought the set, and the children would hurry through their homework so they could read it before bed. By the time DeBakey entered college, he'd read the entire set.

> *You read about somebody else's life, but it makes you think of your own. That's the beauty of it. That's why I love books.*
>
> —*Oprah Winfrey*

DeBakey went on to become Dr. Michael DeBakey, world-famous heart surgeon. Today Dr. DeBakey is 90 years old, yet he shows no signs of slowing down—his daily work still includes operating, teaching, and research. Among DeBakey's achievements: He invented procedures to repair damaged hearts; he developed the first synthetic blood vessels; he has personally operated on more than 60,000 people over the years; and he virtually invented heart bypass surgery, a procedure that saves hundreds of thousands of lives each year!

As an aside, I want you to know that DeBakey is more than just a story in one of my books. His lifelong commitment to growing personally and professionally by reading touched my life in a very personal way. You see, in 1976 my father learned he needed to have open-heart surgery. He sought out the best surgeon in the world to perform the operation. I'm sure you can guess whom he chose to perform the operation—none other than the legendary Dr. Michael DeBakey.

Reading and Research

Obviously, reading paved the way for the DeBakey children to excel in life—Michael's brother is also a surgeon, and his two sisters are highly regarded medical writers. But what I find particularly fascinating about Dr. DeBakey is how he used reading to go beyond learning about the known to discover the unknown! Let me explain:

Back in 1932 when DeBakey was a 24-year-old medical student, his lab supervisor asked him to find a pump that could be used to mimic the human pulse. At the time open-heart surgery was rare, if not impossible, for there was no way to keep the blood pumping while the heart was being repaired.

DeBakey couldn't find any information about pumps in the medical library, so he chose to take the creative approach— he researched pumps in the engineering library! He left his assumptions at the doorstep and researched pumps dating back 2,000 years. He finally discovered a 19th century pump that could be adapted to create the world's first successful heart-lung machine. Modern heart surgery was born!

Look, I'm not so naive as to tell you that you can become the next Dr. Michael DeBakey by reading as a child. For most of us, that's just not going to happen. But there are some valuable lessons about reading that all of us can learn from the DeBakey family.

Leveling the Playing Field

Lesson one: Reading is the great equalizer. We've all experienced situations in which we were the outsider in a group. It's a lonely feeling, all right. There's no question that people who look or talk differently have a harder time making it in this world. But one thing about this country is that we reward excellence. If you can do the job and get results, you're not going to remain an outsider for long, that's for sure.

People who are avid readers, no matter what their background, have an advantage over non-readers, plain and simple. And in an increasingly competitive world, people are more concerned with *what* you know than *who* you know, which wasn't the case 50 or so years ago when family connections carried a lot of weight.

Lesson two: Readers have a world of information at their fingertips if they'll only put forth a little effort to get it. Every time I go into the library I'm amazed at how helpful the staff is and at how much FREE information is available for the asking.

Same goes for the Internet. The worldwide web gives us the world at our fingertips for a few bucks a month. And it's

getting cheaper... and faster... and bigger... and easier to use
by the hour! Unbelievable!

Change Your Life TV

Anyone who has ever tuned in an afternoon TV talk show knows
immediately what the phrase "dummying down" is all about.
All too many of those shows exploit the worst side of human
nature, featuring topics like "mothers who date their daugh-
ters' boyfriends."

You get the idea.

Oprah Winfrey, queen of the talk show hosts, would be the
first to admit that TV is a powerful medium and a great source
of entertainment, but a little TV goes a long way. TV—unlike
reading—doesn't promote personal growth.

"TV promotes false values," she says candidly.

That's why it was such a breath of fresh air when Oprah
decided to turn her back on daytime-trash-TV by starting
Oprah's Book Club, an on-air discussion of a best-selling book.
Books hold a special place in Oprah's heart, for she contends
that it was books, more than any other single influence, that
led to her dramatic success.

Born in Mississippi to a poor, unwed mother, Oprah was
left in the care of her uneducated grandmother, hardly the
kind of nurturing background that would eventually produce
the richest, most powerful personality in television. At age
six, Oprah was sent to live with her father and stepmother in
Nashville, where she experienced a life-altering event: She got
her first library card. It was her father and stepmother who
instilled the priceless value of reading. They even went so far
as to require Oprah to write book reports about what she read.

When a young fan asked her how she became a talk show
host, she replied, "It all started because I was a great reader."

As a youngster Oprah was only allowed to watch one hour
of TV a day, so she turned to books for entertainment... for
company... and for comfort. More than once she has called
books her friends—at times they were her only friends. When
Oprah speaks passionately of the "transformative power of
books," she is speaking from experience. She is speaking from
her heart. She characterizes the power of reading this way:

"You read about somebody else's life, but it makes you think of your own. That's the beauty of it. That's why I love books."

Goal: Get People Reading Again

Oprah is perhaps the single most influential person in the world when it comes to reading. Her program reaches as many as 20 million viewers a day in 130 different countries. And her often-stated goal is to get "the whole country reading again." She openly admits that her real satisfaction with the book club's success is getting people to read for the first time in their adult lives.

She is so satisfied with the success of her book club that she is expanding the format of *The Oprah Winfrey Show* to include week-long discussions with authors of novels and self-help books she has found especially meaningful, such as John Gray's *Men Are From Mars, Women Are From Venus.*

"I want to help people create the highest vision for themselves," she says. Because books have helped transform her life so dramatically, she's not afraid to use her clout to persuade millions of viewers to follow her lead... and read! The most important thing to Winfrey is that people aren't just reading—but *beginning to think about what they have read*!

"It's one thing to win an Emmy," she says. "It's another thing to influence somebody who hasn't picked up a book since they were forced to in high school and for them to start thinking differently about their own life as a result of that."

Oprah's comment sounds a lot like reading and growing rich, doesn't it? And her life is evidence that people can read and grow. Even today Oprah reads religiously every day. She usually has two books going at the same time—a novel and a self-help book. When does a one-woman Fortune 500 company find time to read? Unlike all too many of us, she reads instead of watching TV.

If They Can Do It, You Can Do It

You've just finished reading some pretty remarkable stories about people from all backgrounds who have transformed their lives through reading.

You read about Carol, a young widow who turned to

reading to help her heal and to provide for herself and her two teenagers.

You read about prisoners who are using reading to help them break their criminal cycles and start living responsible, productive lives.

You read about an immigrant family who used reading as a way to compensate for being "outsiders," and, as a result, went on to excel as surgeons and medical writers.

You read about a functionally illiterate 40-year-old minister who succeeded in enriching his spiritual life by learning to read the Bible on his own.

You read about a world-famous talk show host who used reading to rise above her disadvantaged childhood and who uses her popular TV program to "get America reading again."

Although some of these people are rich and famous today, inside they're really no different than you and me. From time to time, we've all felt the emotions the people in these stories have felt. We've all felt shame, like Earl Flowers. We've all felt as if we were an outsider, like Michael DeBakey. We've all felt inferior. We've all felt anger. Self-doubt. Helplessness. Worry. Stress. Depression. And grief.

But the good news is these people didn't give in to the despair of their negative emotions. They recognized they had challenges in their lives, and they turned to reading to help them overcome those challenges.

If reading helped them grow richer in their lives, it stands to reason it can do the same for you.

Reading Releases a Trapped Soul

I'd like to end this chapter with one more story about the transforming power of reading. This story involves a little girl who was dealt a bad hand in life. When she was only a year and a half old, a childhood illness took away her sight and hearing.

The girl was trapped inside her mind. She hadn't learned to speak, so she uttered grunts and animal sounds. She went into unprovoked fits of rage, smashing dishes and physically attacking anyone in the room with her. She snarled while she ate, like a wild animal. More than one doctor diagnosed her as mentally ill. They recommended putting her into an insane asylum for the rest of her life. Her parents refused.

When the girl was seven, the family hired a young woman to tutor her. For weeks the tutor tried to communicate with the girl by spelling words into her hand. The little girl could feel the tutor's fingers on her palm, but the symbols didn't have any meaning to her.

She was still trapped.

Reading Provides a Breakthrough

Then one day there came a breakthrough. The little girl was holding a cup under a gushing water spout. The tutor kept spelling the word "w-a-t-e-r" into the girl's hand.

Suddenly, the little girl understood that the letters represented an object! In that flash of recognition, the door to the world flew wide open to the little girl. She ran around the yard, grabbing objects at random, begging the tutor to spell the name of each object into her palm. As the little girl wrote years later, "Spark after spark of meaning flew from hand to hand." That day the little girl was no longer trapped inside her mind. She was finally free.

This story is a perfect metaphor for all of our lives. At times we've all felt trapped inside our minds, unable to understand or express our true feelings. At times like these we felt alone. Frightened. And angry.

But we don't have to remain that way. Like the little girl, reading can help us break through our mental prison. Reading has the power to transform us by connecting us to others and to ourselves. It's a tool that anyone, including YOU, can use to help you grow to your full potential.

The little girl, by the way, did manage to grow to her full potential, and it was the technology of reading that enabled her to transform herself. Once she understood the concept of reading and writing, she became a voracious learner. By the time she was 10, she was writing letters in French to famous persons in Europe!

She decided to go to college, and her dedicated tutor sat beside her spelling the words of lectures into her hand. She graduated from Radcliffe with honors, and went on to become a celebrated writer who was honored by kings and presidents.

Just think—the little girl's life began when she learned to read.

Her name, by the way, was Helen.

Helen Keller.

10 Writings That Rocked the World

In this chapter we looked at some people who had the wisdom and discipline to read and grow rich in all phases of their lives. These individuals are amazing testimonies to the fact that people can transform their lives by making a conscious choice to read great books.

What's even more amazing is that there are some writings that are so powerful, so compelling, that they have transformed entire cultures and everyone in them—*even though most people have never even read them!* I call these books, plays, poems, and documents "10 writings that rocked the world."

These revolutionary writings have shaped who you are and how you think—even if you've never read them!

In the next chapter, you won't just be reading about 10 great writings.

In the next chapter, you'll be reading about yourself!

7

10 Writings That Rocked the World!

> *In the best of books,*
> *great men talk to us,*
> *give us their most precious thoughts,*
> *and pour their souls into ours.*
> —William Ellery
> Channing

I ENDED THE LAST CHAPTER with a provocative statement that bears repeating: "Some writings are so powerful, so compelling, that they have transformed whole cultures—*even though most people have never read them!*"

"How could that be?" you might ask. "How can a book transform a culture if very few people even read it? Impossible!"

It's not only possible, it's a proven fact. The U.S. Constitution is a perfect example.

Do you know anyone who has read all of the Constitution? I don't. And I doubt if half of the people serving in Congress have read the Constitution all the way through, either. But you and I and every other person in this country conducts every waking minute of our lives according to the laws laid down in the Constitution.

When in Cuba, Do as the Cubans Do—Or Else!

What do you think would happen if an American business-man sat down in a coffee shop in Havana, Cuba, and openly criticized the Cuban government? I'll tell you what would happen—the police would arrest him before he could finish his espresso.

"You didn't read me my rights!" the businessman would prob-ably shout as they hauled him off to jail.

"I have a right to talk to my attorney before answering any ques-tions!" he would likely complain during the interrogation. And when they tossed him into a filthy jail cell, he'd most likely whine, *"Hey, you can't do this—I never got a trial by jury!"*

The point is that the businessman would certainly be aware of his rights under the U.S. Constitution. Only problem is, those rights don't apply in Cuba!

"Oops! Just kidding about the rights thing, Fidel. Can I go home now?"

I can hear the answer all the way over here in Tampa—*CLANG!!!*

Touched by Two Constitutions

I made up the story about the businessman in Cuba to illus-trate the difference between two writings that have dramati-cally impacted the world—the U.S. Constitution and the *Communist Manifesto*! I've never read either of them, but believe me, *they've transformed my life big time*!

You see, 40 years ago my parents lived in Cuba. They owned a dozen businesses and were worth $40 million. Then Castro took over and my parents were forced to flee in the middle of the night, leaving everything they worked for behind. I was born four years later in Puerto Rico and raised in the U.S.

You could say my life has been touched by two constitu-tions—the U.S. Constitution and the Cuban Constitution. But the word *"touched"* doesn't begin to describe the impact they've had on me.

"Rocked" is a more accurate word.

That's why I use the phrase "revolutionary writings that rocked your world" to describe certain breakthrough writings that have dramatically impacted your life, whether you have taken the time to read those writings or not. These writings haven't just "touched" you—they have shaped your attitudes... sculpted your beliefs... defined your values... determined your thoughts... and motivated your actions. If that's not "rocked," I don't know what is!

Writings Shape Who Your Are and How You Think

Like I said, my life had been rocked by two very different writings. In truth, I've been shaped by a lot more than two writings—*and so have you!*

To prove my point, imagine for a moment that you were born and raised in mainland China instead of the U.S. If that were the case, your world would be rocked by the revolutionary writings of Confucius... Buddha... and Mao Tse-Tung. As a result, you would think differently... act differently... even dream differently than you do right now. In fact, if you were raised Chinese, you would BE an entirely different person than you are right now.

> *A drop of ink may make a million think.*
>
> —Lord Byron

Here's why: For centuries the Chinese culture has admired and encouraged conformity. "If the nail stands out, pound it down" is their cultural philosophy. Why? Because 2,500 years ago a brilliant philosopher named Confucius sought to promote peace and unify the country by teaching people to conform to the group rather than stand out. He came up with a system of manners, sayings, and customs designed to put the interests of society above the interests of each individual.

Confucius' disciples wrote down his teachings and circulated them all over China, and they were handed down from generation to generation. The writings of Confucius are a big reason the Chinese continue to play down their individuality. They admire conformity... humility... modesty... patience... tradition... and rituals. Amazingly, 25 centuries after Confucius' revolutionary teachings were first written down, they still continue to rock Chinese culture.

Our culture, on the other hand, was rocked by entirely different writings, such as the Declaration of Independence and the Bill of Rights. These revolutionary writings focused on the individual, as opposed to society at large. As a result, our culture rewards individualism. We admire people who are different... who have the courage to create their own destiny... who forge their own path. Why? Because the writings that rocked our world tell us that individualism is a good thing.

Different writings.
Different cultures.
Different you.

The Medium Is the Message

Do you think the teachings of Confucius and the principles outlined in the Declaration of Independence would have had the same cultural impact if they hadn't been written down?

Of course not!

But because they were recorded in writing, they could be read... copied... circulated... studied... pondered... discussed... debated... added to... amended... and adapted, so that today they still have the power to rock the world.

Can you think of any other medium other than writing that has the power to transform whole hemispheres? Has there ever been a movie... or a symphony... or a painting... with the power to turn the tide of history as much as the written word? No way!

I'm not saying these other media haven't had a dramatic impact on people. Of course they have. But the impact of a powerful movie, such as *Schindler's List;* or a powerful TV show, such as *Roots*, can't compare to the impact of a powerful written text.

Think about it. For a movie or a TV program to dramatically influence a culture, it must be viewed by a big percentage of the population, as was the case with *Schindler's List*. But this isn't the case with powerful writings, which are burned like a brand into the collective consciousness of a culture, even if very few people take the time to read those writings.

Writings That Rocked the World

In the rest of this chapter, we're going to take a brief look at 10 writings that rocked the world. These writings have charted the course of Western civiliza- tion. Just as a printed chart guides the course for a huge ocean liner and all of the passengers onboard, these writings have determined the direction of your life, whether you have read them or not.

Only three things are necessary to make life happy: the blessing of God, books, and a friend.

—Lacordaire

Some of these documents are thousands of years old. Others are only a few decades old. Whether ancient or recent, they have all dramatically changed the course of your life for one main reason —*they were all written down!* If they hadn't been, the content would have been lost to the ages.

But because these documents were recorded in writing, each generation could read and study them and then pass them along to the next generation, which enabled certain writings to shape the outcome of history... and shape the way you and I think and act every single day!

1. The Bible
(4,000 BC – AD 100)

Let's begin with a collection of writings that rocked the world more than any other writings in history—the Bible.

This discussion isn't about religion, per se. Whether you're a Christian... a Jew... a Moslem... a Hindu... or an atheist isn't the issue here. The issue is the impact the Bible has had in shaping Western civilization, and, as a result, in shaping *who you are... how you think... and how you act.*

The Bible is the wellspring of Western civilization. For thousands of years it has shaped our values and guided our laws. It tells us how to behave. It defines right and wrong. It teaches us lessons. It tells us timeless stories. It sets down rules of conduct. It tells us how the world came about... where we humans came from... and where we're going after we die. It continues to dominate the bestseller lists year in and year out. No other book is even close.

Reading Bible stories that teach timeless lessons empowers us to make better choices, and, as a result, become better people. When we read the story of Cain and Abel, we learn to avoid the pitfalls of envy. When we read the story of Job, we learn the value of faith and hope. When we read the story of David, we're reminded of the power of dreaming big dreams and overcoming great odds.

That's why the Bible has just as much relevance today as it did thousands of years ago—it's a prescription for righteous living. The Ten Commandments are just as applicable today as they were when Moses carried them down from Mt. Sinai 3,500 years ago.

2. The Ancient Greek Philosophers
(350 – 450 BC)

One afternoon a young poet named Plato was walking down a street in Athens, Greece, when he struck up a conversation with an eccentric, barefooted philosopher named Socrates. Plato went home a changed man. He tore up all of his poems and decided on the spot to follow in Socrates' footsteps and become a philosopher.

The books that help you most are those which make you think the most.

—Theodore Parker

Several years later Plato opened a school to teach other bright, young philosophers, among them a brilliant student named Aristotle, who, in turn, became a tutor to Alexander the Great. Amazingly, in the span of 100 years, three giant Greek philosophers and several brilliant Greek playwrights created the writings that would form one of the two pillars of Western civilization, the second pillar being the Bible.

How important were the writings of the Greek philosophers? Let me put it this way: Think of Western civilization as a vast, beautiful flower garden. Now think of the Greek philosophers as the soil. Their writings laid the groundwork for our institutions of justice, politics, government, education, science, commerce, and the arts. (If I missed anything worthwhile, you can probably add it to the list, too.)

3. The Magna Carta
(1215)

Almost eight centuries ago, during the Middle Ages, the most influential legal document in Western civilization was reluctantly signed and sealed by King John, a greedy, over-reaching monarch who abused his power and brutally exploited his subjects.

The barons finally got together and said, "Enough is enough!" They demanded that King John sign a written document guaranteeing them certain "rights." The document became known as the Magna Carta, which is Latin for "the great charter."

And a great charter it was, for the Magna Carta was the first recorded attempt by the citizens of a land (other than the ancient Greeks) to broaden their civil rights and limit the power of the government. It became the forerunner of the U.S. Constitution (and, therefore, the forerunner for the constitution of every major country in the world), and set down the key laws and liberties that we enjoy today, including trial by jury and the concept of civil rights.

When I get a little money, I buy books; and if any is left, I buy food and clothes.

—*Erasmus*

When you consider the power that kings had back in the Middle Ages, the Magna Carta was a breakthrough document in that it established rights that were eventually extended to common citizens, like you and me. God bless the Magna Carta!

4. The Gutenberg Bible
(1440)

Johannes Gutenberg couldn't have anticipated how his invention would rock the world. All he wanted to do is print a few Bibles and make a few bucks. But the invention of the printing press, perhaps more than any invention other than writing itself, opened the door for the masses (that's you and me, folks) to have access to the same information that was formerly reserved to the powerful few. The mass marketing of books led to mass awareness, which in turn led to mass sharing of knowledge and information.

Because of Gutenberg's press, the concept of reading and growing rich was no longer the private domain of the privileged and the powerful. A commoner could enjoy the same literature as a nobleman... could read the same Bible as the officials of the church... could study the same science books as the children of the aristocrats. In short, the printing press leveled the playing field between the rich and the poor.

5. Martin Luther's 95 Theses
(1517)

No one took much notice in 1517 when a 34 year old monk named Martin Luther walked up the steps of the Catholic church in Wittenberg, Germany, until he began nailing his 95 Theses to the church door. Who would have guessed that the pounding of that single nail would echo around the world for centuries to come?

I have sought for happiness everywhere, but I have found it nowhere except in a little corner with a little book.

—*Thomas à Kempis*

What started out as a protest (the word "protestant" comes from the word "protest") against the policies of Pope Leo X ended up leading to one of the biggest power shifts in history. Luther encouraged everyone, not just church officials, to read and interpret the Bible for themselves, and his "heretical" teachings led to the formation of Protestantism.

Americans are especially indebted to Luther, for 103 years after he nailed his 95 Theses to a church door, a small denomination who called themselves the "Puritans" decided to flee to America where they would be free to practice their own unique brand of Protestantism.

The rest, as they say, is history—*our history*!

6. Shakespeare's Plays and Sonnets
(1564-1616)

The plays and sonnets of William Shakespeare are the second-most quoted writings in the world after the Bible.

To date 250,000 books about Shakespeare or his plays have
been published, and the number of papers and essays would
easily number into the millions.

No other author even comes
close to having the impact and
popularity of William Shakespeare.
Every American who ever attended
high school can remember struggling through *Romeo and Juliet*,
MacBeth, or *Julius Caesar*, and if you
were fortunate enough to have an
English teacher who could breathe
life into his brilliant metaphors,
you'll understand why he's still regarded as the world's greatest
writer.

> *Powerful writings
> are burned like a brand
> into the collective con-
> sciousness of a culture,
> even if very few people
> take the time to read
> those writings.*
>
> —Burke Hedges

Shakespeare's writings continue to rock the world because anyone who reads Shakespeare—no matter how much
or how little money they have in the bank—will grow richer
in wisdom and in their appreciation for his mastery of the
English language.

7. The Declaration of Independence
(1776)

On July 4, 1776, 56 men assembled in a hot, muggy room
in Philadelphia to ratify a written document that would send a
long-overdue message that from this day forth, *governments
would rule by the consent of the governed*. It was the beginning of
the end for monarchies and dictators the world over.

The Declaration of Independence was mostly the work of
one man, Thomas Jefferson, who wrote the bulk of the document in two days without notes or reference material. His
eloquence was such that the opening sentence sums up the
core philosophy of virtually every citizen in America:

> *"We hold these truths to be self-evident, that all men are cre-
> ated equal, that they are endowed by their Creator with cer-
> tain unalienable rights, that among these are Life, Liberty
> and the pursuit of Happiness."*

8. U.S. Constitution and the Bill of Rights
(1787-1791)

Here's a little-known fact that I think is astounding: The U.S. Constitution is the oldest written constitution among the major countries of the world.

Isn't that amazing? It's only 200 or so years old and it's the oldest constitution in the world. *Wow—talk about a paradigm shift!*

Prior to the ratification of the U.S. Constitution in 1787, the world was ruled by the whims of kings, dictators, powerful war lords, and tribal chiefs. In the 200 years since, virtually every nation on Earth has adopted a written constitution, and it's no coincidence that the majority of these nations—and every single one of the democratic nations— looked to the U.S. Constitution as a blueprint for creating their own governments.

9. Communist Manifesto
(1848)

The writings that you've read about up to this point rocked the world in the best sense of the word—to use President Bush's words, they made the world a "kinder, gentler place."

But, sadly, that's not the case with the last two writings you'll read about, the *Communist Manifesto* and *Mein Kampf*. These two writings brought about suffering... destruction... and death on a scale never witnessed before, proving that writings can also have the power to rock the world in ugly and destructive ways.

Karl Marx and Friedrich Engels outlined the platform for implementing their half-baked theories in a short booklet entitled, the *Communist Manifesto*. The document advocated the surrender of private property and the end to all existing institutions. Communism spread like wildfire, and heartless dictators like Stalin in Russia... Mao in China... and Pol Pot in Cambodia murdered as many as 100 million innocent people during the 20th century and imprisoned millions more—and the terror continues to this day!

10. Mein Kampf
(1927)

Mein Kampf means "my struggle," and Adolf Hitler wrote most of his twisted philosophy of Aryan superiority during his imprisonment for leading an uprising against the German government.

Hitler used *Mein Kampf* to spread the message that people could help themselves by hating others, and, tragically, a majority of the German people bought into his crackpot theories with these tragic results: Six million Jews died in concentration camps, along with several million Catholics, Gypsies, artists, mental patients (and virtually anyone else who didn't fit into Hitler's idea of the "ideal German"). All told, 55 million people lost their lives during WWII.

Mein Kampf proves that the written word has the power to corrupt and impoverish readers just as much as it has the power to enhance our lives and help us grow rich. As I point out in a later chapter, *you are what you read—so be careful what you read!*

There you have it—10 writings that rocked the world... 10 writings that are so powerful they have shaped entire cultures—*whether most people have read them or not!*

Like I said earlier, you can't say that about a TV show. Or a movie. Or an audio tape.

If books have the power to change entire cultures, just think what a book can do for one single person... *just think what a book can do for you!*

That's why I tell people that their best edge in the new economy is still the old technology—books!

8

Reading & Writing:
The Greatest Technology
Ever Invented!

*Not to be able to read is like one world with
one door to enter and nothing is there....
Because of literacy, I have been freed from
this dark world. Because of literacy, I have
1,000 doors that I can enter now.*

—Ernest Carr
former student at
Memphis Literacy Council

T RY TO IMAGINE A WORLD without reading and writing.

There wouldn't be any books, newspapers, or magazines—
that's obvious. But that's only the beginning.

Without reading and writing, there would be no TV. No
movies. No pencils or pens. No paper. No street signs. No
addresses. No contracts. No stock market. No dictionaries.
No shopping lists. No mail. No libraries. No cars. No bi-
cycles. No factories. No signs. No phone books. No phones.
No city hall. No professional sports. No grocery stores (no
stores, period). No banks. No checks. No printed money.
No maps. No schools. No calendars. No clocks. No watches.
No airplanes. No typewriters. No computers.

In short, no civilization as we know it. And no progress, to speak of.

Without reading and writing, we'd be stuck in the Stone Age.

Activating Human Potential

I call reading and writing the greatest technology ever invented because it gave us humans the key to unlock our hidden potential. If you don't think so, just look at the opening list again. If certifiable geniuses, such as Einstein... or Mozart... or Shakespeare... were born before the invention of writing, would they have ever realized their genius potential? Not a chance! They'd have been too busy trying to survive to sit around and think great thoughts or create great works of art. All that great potential would have gone to waste, and the world would be poorer for it.

Reading and writing liberates us and activates our dormant minds, much like a catalyst activates an inert chemical solution. Without the catalyst, the chemical just sits there. Add the catalyst and—BOOM!—there's an explosion of activity.

Chiseling Away the Rough Edges

To better illustrate my point, I'd like to tell you a true story that happened several hundred years ago. A young Italian sculptor named Agostino had a huge block of marble delivered to his studio. He had great plans to sculpt the block into a marvelous statue, but, unfortunately, he found the marble hard to work with. Frustrated, he had the marble removed to make room for a different project.

> *If a book we are reading doesn't shake us awake like a blow to the skull, why bother reading it?*
>
> —Franz Kafka

Forty years later another Italian sculptor named Michelangelo spotted the marble block hidden in the weeds of an abandoned garbage heap. He ordered it sent to his studio.

Michelangelo studied the marble block for weeks, sizing up its potential. He measured it again and again. Tested its

hardness with his chisels. And made endless sketches. Then
he went to work. Three years later he chiselled away the last
of the marble block and gently smoothed his completed statue.

It was the statue of David.

You see, Michelangelo did what Agostino failed to do—he
saw the full potential of the marble block and released that
potential with his talent and his chisels.

This story applies to humans as much as it does to blocks
of marble. We're coarse and rough and unrefined at first, but
we have such great potential! Reading is the chisel that releases our full potential. Reading helps us chip away the rough
edges and reveal the work of art within. Without his chisels,
Michelangelo could never have created his masterpiece. And
without reading and writing, humans could never have activated their full human potential.

What's So Magical About Reading and Writing?

"What's so magical about reading and writing?" you may be
thinking. "There's no difference between watching a TV program on Winston Churchill or reading about him in a book—
either way, I get the information, right?"

Wrong.

Look—I didn't call this book *Watch TV and Grow Rich...* or
Listen and Grow Rich... or *Talk and Grow Rich* for good reason.
Our five senses—smelling, seeing, hearing, touching, and tasting—enable us to explore and understand ourselves and our
world *physically*. But reading enables us to explore and understand ourselves and our world *intellectually*. And that makes all
the difference!

You see, something happens when we read that doesn't
happen when we get information in other ways. Remember
the subtitle of this book:

How *the hidden powers of reading* can make you richer in all
areas of your life.

The phrase "the hidden power of reading" is the key to
understanding what sets reading apart from every other human activity. Those "hidden powers" can transform us like
nothing else. And they can help us grow rich in all areas of
our lives.

In the next few pages I'll do my best to explain WHAT the hidden powers of reading are and WHY those powers—and those powers alone—can activate our full human potential. A word of caution: Some of the information you're about to read is a little lofty—so bear with me if I sound a little "textbooky" from time to time.

Non-Reading Cultures Are Frozen in Time

The best way to truly appreciate this amazing technology called reading and writing is to briefly look at how literacy came about and how it has changed civilization.

Before the written word, cultures were frozen in time. Non-literate cultures, often referred to as "oral cultures," have been known to remain unchanged for thousands of years, as evidenced by several small hunter-gatherer tribes still eking out an existence in the Amazon rain forest.

> *Words are, of course,*
> *the most powerful*
> *drug used by*
> *mankind.*
>
> —Rudyard Kipling

Dr. Walter Ong, a world-famous expert in oral and written cultures, estimates that there have been tens of thousands of different languages throughout history, but only 106 were ever written down. Of the 3,000 or so languages spoken today, only 78 have developed written literature, that is, stories, poems, and plays.

Dr. Ong goes on to say that every oral culture he knows of wants to learn to read and write as soon as possible. It seems that oral cultures understand the value of recording their language, recognizing that what is unwritten, no matter how wise or profound, is eventually lost through disuse or alteration.

That's why I say writing is the greatest technology ever invented. The technology of reading and writing gave cultures a powerful tool whereby they could leverage their spoken language to make it a thousand times more productive. Reading and writing allowed early humans to make a quantum leap into the modern world.

How Reading Activates the Human Potential

Most experts agree that writing was invented almost 6,000

years ago in either Egypt or an area now known as Iraq or Iran. Somewhere around 700 BC, the Greeks shaped their writing system into the 24 symbols that we now call an "alphabet" (the word "alphabet" comes from the first two letters of the Greek alphabet, *alpha* and *beta*).

At first writing was mainly used as a way to keep better records. Writing allowed merchants to keep track of grain and livestock; it allowed citizens to draw up contracts; and it allowed governments to keep track of taxes and record laws.

Over several centuries the Greeks discovered more and more uses for writing and reading, and eventually the politicians and wealthy merchants started using writing as a tool to help them compose and remember their speeches. And the Greeks loved making speeches!

Speech-making was how the Greeks communicated ideas... governed their city-states... settled disagreements... and entertained themselves. Speech contests were even part of their Olympic Games. To be known as a great speaker was one of the highest achievements in ancient Greece.

By 350 BC, virtually all of the great thinkers and politicians in Athens were literate. Writing and reading enabled them to compose and refine their own material and to rehearse and memorize their speeches before appearing in public. Eventually, every prominent citizen, as well as many slaves, learned to read and write. And the more literacy took hold, the more the Greeks activated their human potential. It's no coincidence that the greatest thinkers, philosophers, and playwrights in ancient Greece could all read and write.

Ironically, the ancient Greeks didn't understand the liberating power of reading and writing, even though their writings laid the groundwork for liberating the world! Socrates and Plato, for example, argued that a speaker was superior to the written text because writing couldn't defend itself or elaborate when a reader challenged it. But Socrates and Plato, great thinkers that they were, failed to understand the hidden power of reading and writing—they failed to understand that reading and writing had the power to expand human potential by *transforming the way we think*!

Reading and Writing Expand Our Mental Powers

We now know that certain powerful patterns of thought remain dormant in people until they mentally internalize the complex process of reading and writing. It's as if literacy were a powerful hormone that could magically activate our minds so that we can *grow* to our full intellectual potential. Dr. Ong puts it this way:

> *Without writing, the literate mind would not and could not think as it does... even when its composing its thoughts in oral form. More than any other single invention, writing has transformed human consciousness.*

According to Dr. Ong, the thinking patterns of oral cultures are less versatile than those of literate cultures. The people in oral cultures don't arrange their thoughts in some fundamental mental patterns that literate people have come to rely on.

Oral cultures, for example, don't arrange their thoughts in terms of comparing and contrasting or cause and effect. They don't think in terms of definitions and categorizing. They don't spend time in self-analysis. They don't conjure up geometrical shapes in their minds or follow logical reasoning processes. They don't think in terms of discovering by "conducting research." They don't seek to confirm existing knowledge or discover new knowledge by "looking something up"... "researching the facts" ... "doing your due diligence"... and "thinking out of the box"... as literate cultures do.

Oral Cultures and the Status Quo

By their very nature, oral cultures are conservative and resistant to change, for their goal isn't to seek new truths or to challenge tradition, but to preserve it. Oral cultures have learned to rely on mental devices that make it easier to remember and pass their culture along to each generation. This is why so much of the talk in oral cultures centers around listing... repetition... rhyming... proverbs... old sayings... and common stories about brave ancestors.

The language of the Old Testament is a perfect example. Much of what is written in the Old Testament was handed down orally for thousands of years before literate Jewish scribes recorded it. When you read in Chronicles I:37-38 that "... Za-bad begat Eph-lal, and Eph-lal begat O-bed. And O-bed begat Je-hu, and Je-hu begat Az-a-ri-ah," and so on, you are witnessing the way members of an oral culture use listing and repetition to help them remember their genealogy so they can pass it along to their offspring.

Free thinkers such as Socrates, who went around challenging people's basic values and assumptions, seldom exist in oral cultures.

> *When I am reading a book, whether wise or silly, it seems to me to be alive and talking to me.*
>
> —Jonathan Swift

And if people like Socrates do exist in an oral culture, they are often killed or banished because they threaten the oral tradition. Little wonder that Socrates was convicted of "corrupting the youth of Athens" and condemned to death. His literate approach to thinking and solving problems was much too threatening to the Greek politicians because most of them were still mentally married to an oral culture.

The Questions We Ask When We Read

The greatest Greek philosophers, writers, and mathematicians came up with a whole new way of looking at the world because reading and writing expanded their minds and gave them fresh, new perspectives through which to view the world. Even though 2,000 years separate us from the great thinkers, reading still has the power to transform us by activating more of our potential.

Take a moment to review your thought processes as you read this book. While you were reading the previous paragraphs, your mind was flashing back and forth between agreeing with what I said to criticizing... evaluating... defending... comparing... challenging... clarifying... pondering... testing... disagreeing... and so on. Cultures that don't read don't bother with these types of mental gymnastics.

But we just take these sophisticated mental functions for granted. We don't consciously try to think in a certain way when we read. It's second nature to us. It's hidden until someone brings it to our attention. We can think about a written message in ways that oral people could never think about a spoken message because reading releases those hidden powers in our minds. In short, when we read and write, we open doors that empower us to perform mental functions that we couldn't perform before, which, in turn, enables us to tap more fully into our human potential. And when we use more of our innate, God-given potential, we're growing rich.

Now are you beginning to understand what the expression, "Read and grow rich" really means? Not *hear* and grow rich. Not *talk* and grow rich. But READ and grow rich!

Feudal Japan: Frozen in Time

When I started this chapter, I made the statement that oral cultures remain frozen in time. The best example is ancient Japan. Japan's dramatic transformation from a static, isolated fuedal state to a dynamic, international super power is a testimony to the power of reading and writing.

Like Europe, Japan came out of a feudal tradition. Europe had kings, Japan had emperors. Europe had barons, Japan had shoguns. Europe had knights, Japan had samurai warriors. In the early 1600s, Japan decided to preserve its culture by ridding itself of all foreign influences. All western inventions, including guns, were banned. All foreigners, including Christian missionaries, were kicked out. A few literate, rich shoguns ruled millions of illiterate poor peasants with an iron hand. And for the next 250 years, this system remained unchanged.

Japan was frozen in time.

Commodore Perry Breaks the Ice

In 1853 Commodore Perry's squadron of four steamships chugged into Tokyo Bay and demanded that isolationist Japan trade with the outside world. The shocked Japanese had never seen anything like Perry's fleet, calling his steamships "floating volcanoes." The U.S. Navy's exhibition of technical superiority shocked the Japanese shoguns into admitting that Japan had to join the 20th century or get left behind. Soon after Perry's visit, Japan opened its ports and began modernizing by consolidating the country and phasing out the privileges of the feudal nobility.

By the late 1800s, Japan had adopted a written constitution and made education for the masses compulsory. By 1905, 95% of Japanese children were in state-run schools, and within one generation Japan's literacy rate was one of the highest in the world. By 1915, only 60 years after Commodore Perry forced open the doors to its closed culture, Japan was recognized by the West as a major world power.

Japan Reads and Grows Rich

Now, let me ask you a question. If Japan hadn't made a national effort to teach millions of peasant children to read and write, do you think the country could have transformed itself from an ancient, isolated culture into a modern, international super power in 60 years?

There's no way!

Oh, sure, Japan used its *illiterate peasants* to build its modern infra-structure by putting in roads... installing telephone lines... and laying down the railroad tracks. But it was the peasant's *literate children* who read and grew rich. The literate children grew up to become accountants, CEOs, businessmen, politicians, educators, and bankers, and they are the ones who ushered Japan into the 20th century. If Japan didn't have the foresight to teach the masses to read and write, it would have developed more along the lines of China than the U.S. and other modern industrialized nations.

Are You Frozen in Time?

"What's a history lesson on Japan have to do with me?" you may ask.

Everything.

Here's my point: If an *entire culture* can transform itself in a few short decades through the technology of reading and writing, just think what it can do for a *single individual*!

If Japan can read and grow rich, doesn't it stand to reason that you can, too?

Japan chose to remain frozen in time until Commodore Perry thawed the ice of their self-contentment. He opened their eyes to the fact the rest of the world was sailing into the 20th century, and they either had to change... or be changed.

To Japan's credit, they had the wisdom and the discipline to change by taking advantage of the greatest technology ever invented. They chose to read and grow rich.

More than any other single invention, writing has transformed human consciousness.

—Dr. Walter Ong

Well, there's a "virtual" Commodore Perry steaming into our lives right now. But instead of the U.S. Navy bearing down on us, it's the ships of the Information Age carrying a cargo of "future shock" and rapid change into our lives. We can ignore (or worse, deny) the "floating volcanoes" and pretend they'll go away. Or we can do what Japan did—we can activate our full potential by reading and growing.

Like Japan, we can change or be changed. The choice is ours. We can refuse to grow, spending our time watching TV and listening to the radio, choosing to remain frozen in an oral culture of our own making.

Or we can grow, spending our time reading and activating our full mental potential, choosing to take advantage of an ever-changing "e-world" exploding with information and opportunity.

As for me, I made a lifetime commitment to read and grow rich nearly 12 years ago when my sister-in-law handed me a copy of *The Greatest Salesman in the World*.

I've never regretted that decision for one second.

And neither will you.

9

Inside the Mind of a Reader

> *A book must be the axe for the*
> *frozen sea within us.*
> —Franz Kafka

A CATHOLIC MONK NAMED Dom Perignon is credited with accidently discovering the sparkling white wine we call champagne.

When the first sip of the bubbly wine exploded in Dom Perignon's mouth, he was so startled by the carbonated taste that he shouted to his fellow friars:

"Brothers, come quickly—I'm tasting stars!"

Anyone who has ever sipped champagne to celebrate a special occasion would agree that "tasting stars" is an apt metaphor to describe the experience. It's also an apt metaphor for what happens in the minds of readers when they come across a well-turned phrase or a great insight in a book.

Reading great insights is the mental equivalent of "tasting stars."

From Sight to Insight

Have you ever read a sentence or paragraph that contains such a profound nugget of truth that it just jumps off the page and hits you right between the eyes—BAM?

"That's exactly what I've been thinking but could never put into words!" you might say to yourself.

"I never thought of it that way before. That's so true! That's it!"

When I emptied the top drawer of my mind, I found a book.

—George Jessel

Every reader has experienced special moments like these when we're instantly transformed by the written word. Those moments of insight wake us from our slumber of self-contentment and push us to grow, much like a plant bursting through the darkness of the soil and stretching toward the sunlight.

Author Dorothea Brande describes the experience this way:

> *I found the idea which set me free. I was not consciously looking for it. I was engaged on a piece of research in a different field. But I came across a sentence in a book I was reading which was so illuminating that I put the book aside to consider all of the ideas suggested by that [one sentence]. When I picked the book up again, I was a different person.*

"I was a different person." What a great line that is! I know exactly what Dorothea Brande means because that's what happened to me when I finished reading *The Greatest Salesman in the World*—I was a different person.

Brande's observation captures the essence of *Read and Grow Rich*. We've all read something that was so touching or so illuminating that it instantly changed the way we looked at the world. It has happened to me lots of times.

That's one of the hidden powers of reading. It can transform us and make us different—and better— than we were only a few minutes earlier. And when we're getting better, we're growing richer, aren't we?

Reading: The Mental Miracle

Mark Twain was once asked to explain the concept of a miracle.
He paused before replying, "It's a miracle I don't melt every
time I take a bath.'" Twain's wry observation won't win any
science awards, but it does point out a universal truth. Some things are so complex
and mysterious they're much easier to experience than to explain.

Reading is like that. The process of
looking at little black symbols on a white
page and making meaning out of them is
incredibly complex and doesn't lend itself to a simple explanation.

*Reading is
to the mind
what exercise is
to the body.*

—Anonymous

Have you ever stopped to think what happens inside your
mind when you read? I've been an avid reader for 12 years
now, and I didn't even consider that question until I began to
research this book. What I learned amazed and fascinated
me, and it gave me a new-found respect for the complexity of
the physical and mental process that we call reading.

During the rest of this chapter, we're going to examine
the hidden powers of reading. You'll learn the answers to
some key questions, including: What happens inside our minds
when we read? What is it about reading that enables it to
transform lives? What makes reading different from watching
TV or listening to a speech or an audio tape?

What Happens to Us Physically When We Read?

Let's start by briefly examining what happens to us physically
when we read. Prior to my research, I used to think my eyes
traveled smoothly from the left side of the page to the right
when I read. Not true.

Amazingly, when we read our eyes jump 100 to 200 degrees
across the page three to four times per second. These jerks are so
fast that we don't even notice them. The actual reading takes
place during the brief pauses between those jumps, for it's during the pauses that the images of the printed symbols are sent to
our brains, where they are decoded into meaning.

This process of decoding is incredibly complex and light-
ning fast. In fact, reading is every bit as complex as thinking,

which is why the classic textbook, *The Psychology of Reading*, defines reading as "visually guided thinking." Consider a few of the mental functions that occur almost simultaneously as you are reading these sentences.

You see markings on a page and decipher patterns (single words or a multi-word phrase) stored in your memory. You decode those markings... assign mental pictures to them... and then store those pictures into your short-term memory in the time it takes to snap your fingers. Then you scan back and forth between your short-term and long-term memory for experiences or associations that you can attach to these new mental pictures.

> *The real purpose of books is to trap the mind into doing its own thinking.*
>
> —Christopher Morley

When you read the word W-I-N-D in this sentence, for example, you look to the written context to tell you whether the word represents the "*wind* blowing through the leaves" or "*wind* your alarm clock before bed." During the few seconds it takes to read the opening phrase of this paragraph, the neurons in your brain are exploding like popcorn in a popper, performing complex mental functions at lightning-fast speed, such as remembering... imagining... reasoning... connecting... reviewing... hypothesizing... testing via trial and error... all the while cross-checking the printed symbols against your knowledge of grammar and spelling, personal experiences, memories, possible interpretations, false starts, and re-readings. Whew!

And to think all of this takes place in the blink of an eye. Miraculous!

Making Written Text Our Own

What I've just described represents just one level of the reading process. As we become more experienced readers, we expand our mental repertoire to include more sophisticated "visually guided thinking." As we read we may agree or disagree... sympathize... criticize... laugh... memorize... repeat... absorb... scorn... document... adopt... attack, and so on. In other words, we test what we read to see which written messages we'll add to our own philosophy and which ones we'll throw out. At this stage we're not just reading words for meaning. We're making the text our own.

If all of these mental gymnastics seem like a lot of work, well, you're right. When you read you're making a big investment in time and effort. And that investment is precisely what makes reading such a valuable activity.

You see, unlike watching TV or listening to someone talk, reading requires a higher degree of mental participation because we have to actively create and recreate meaning. When we watch TV, we don't need to use very much of our imagination. The moving pictures and the soundtrack fill up our senses, reducing our mental participation. TV is a medium that encourages us to be passive.

When we read, on the other hand, we have to *create* our own mental pictures. We control the pace. We stop and reread. We sort and check any new information against what we already know. Like a sculptor shaping clay, we shape the text we are reading—pressing hard on some parts while smoothing over others. That's what I mean when I say we make the text our own.

We Value What We Earn

Funny thing about human nature—we all look for shortcuts and seek the easy way out, but the things that we value the most in life are the things we work for. Ever notice that the toys your parents *gave you* were the ones you left at a friend's house or forgot in the rain? But the toys you *bought yourself with your hard-earned money* were the ones you took care of, isn't that true? The same can be said for investing in reading.

It's like the story about the spoiled little rich girl who wanted a new Corvette for her 16th birthday. She kept telling her father—a conservative, self-made millionaire—that nothing other than a Corvette would do for her 16th birthday. She would just DIE unless she got that Corvette!

When the little rich girl came home from school on the day of her birthday, the father greeted her at the front door, hugged her, and said, "Honey, I got you something very special for your birthday. It's in the garage. Why don't you go take a peek at it?"

The girl rushed into the garage, flung the door open wide, and stopped dead in her tracks, a shocked look on her face. There was a brand new, bright red Corvette in the garage, alright. But it had been totally stripped down and disassembled, including the engine. The separate parts were scattered all over the garage floor!

Sitting on the hood of the Corvette was a set of car keys, along with the business card of a mechanic and this scribbled note from her dad:

"Happy birthday! Call this mechanic to help you put the car back together. When you're done, it's all yours! Love, Dad."

Here's the best part of the story: The girl and the mechanic worked nights and weekends for three months to reassemble the Corvette. When it was finally completed, the little rich girl, grinning from ear to ear, backed her shiny red Corvette slowly out of the garage. No one has ever been prouder of a car.

To no one's surprise, the little rich girl took fabulous care of her first car. She kept it spotless. No one drove it but her. And when she grew up, got married, and had children of her own, guess what car she still drove? You guessed it—a 15-year-old red Corvette in perfect condition.

Earning Knowledge the Old-Fashioned Way

This story points out a universal truth—we value what we work for. That's what happens when we get our information from reading books, too—we value it more. Unlike TV programs or videos, reading takes work. We have to concentrate. We have to use our imagination. We have to make an effort. As a result, we place more value on what we learn from reading because the mental investment is greater.

Now, please don't misunderstand me—I'm not saying you can't learn anything from speeches, videos, and audio tapes... or even TV, for that matter. They're all great sources of information. But have you ever noticed how much more you remember when you *write notes* during a speech —and then *read those notes* a few days later? Why? Because when we write things down and read them later, we're performing the mental equivalent of taking our Corvette apart and reassembling it. In other words, we're making the text our own.

Making a Book Our Own

Years ago the great American writer Ernest Hemingway recognized that reading good books creates a special sense of ownership in the reader. Here's what he said:

> *All good books are alike in that they are much truer than if they really happen and after you are finished reading one, you will feel that it all happened to you, and afterwards it all belongs to you.*

That's why we feel so much more fulfilled after reading a book than we do after watching a TV program or listening to an audio. When we read a book, it "belongs to us" because we earned it. I get a deeper satisfaction from finishing a book than I've ever gotten from watching a video or a movie, and the message sticks with me longer.

> *One reads in order to ask questions.*
> —Franz Kafka

It's obvious that our entire culture places a greater value on reading as a way of gathering information than any other medium. Reading has become such an integral part of the way we think that it has spawned dozens of common expressions that we use every day. Here are a just few that come readily to mind:

Read you like a book.

Read 'em and weep (poker players' expression).

Read between the lines.

Get a read on things.

Read the defense (sports metaphor).

Palm reader.

Your life is an open book.

Book of love.

See the writing on the wall.

Read the terrain.

Read my expression.

These many metaphors prove that reading has been internalized and elevated to such a degree in our culture that it has become a part of our subconscious thinking. In other words, reading is such a big part of our lives that we can't even think without thinking about reading!

The great comedian George Jessel put it this way: "When I emptied the top drawer of my mind, I found a book."

Notice he didn't find a movie. Or a song. Or a speech. He found a book.

10

You Are What You Read
(so be careful what you read)

Reading is the loom on which
one's inner garments are woven.
Shoddy reading clothes both
mind and heart in shoddy garments.
—A.P. Gouthey

I'M LOOKING AT A *Family Circus* cartoon by Bill Keane that says a lot about the biggest challenge facing us in the Information Age. Let me describe the cartoon for you.

Three-year-old Dolly is kneeling on her bed saying her goodnight prayers. Her hands are clasped under her chin. Her eyes are closed, and her face is turned upward toward the sky. Her prayer reads, "... *lead us not into temptation, but deliver us from e-mail....*"

I chuckle at Dolly's misunderstanding of the Lord's Prayer, as she mistakenly substitutes the word "e-mail" for the word "evil." But the more I look at the cartoon, the more I realize there is another interpretation. This seemingly innocent cartoon captures the essence of a very adult problem in the Information Age—information overload. We all complain about the amount of "junk mail" we have to contend with. But e-mail messages already outnumber regular mail by 10 to one, and the Internet is just getting started! All we know is the future will bring more, not less, information overload.

In the coming pages we're going to take a closer look at information overload—what it is... what's causing it... and what it means to you and me. Then we'll talk about some strategies for filtering out harmful or useless information while keeping information that can help us grow richer in our lives.

Information Overload: Challenge of the 21st Century

"Deliver us from e-mail" could easily become the slogan of the 21st century. It's not that e-mail is a bad thing. E-mail is great! It's just that e-mail is symbolic of the rising tide of information that we all have to contend with.

Do you have any idea how many e-mail messages are sent every year? Would you guess 10 million? How about a billion? 100 billion? The answer will amaze you. *Today more than one trillion e-mail messages are sent and received each year... and that number is expected to quadruple in the next few years, as seven people gain Internet access every second!*

Let's face it—we're struggling to keep from drowning in a swelling tidal wave of information. We're treading in a sea of junk mail... mail order catalogs (there are 37,000 catalogs in the U.S.)... legal documents... memos and reports... radio and TV advertisements... infomercials... faxes... phone calls... voice mail messages... billboards... e-mail and worldwide web sites... 100-plus TV channels (and growing)... and on and on.

We've even come up with several terms to describe this phenomenon of too much information and too little time to process it all. Here are a few of the more popular ones:

Information overload.

Info-glut.

Infomania.

Information anxiety.

The information explosion.

Data smog.

All of these newly coined words and phrases indicate that we're overwhelmed with information today, which is a pretty ironic statement considering that well into the 20th century, *information scarcity* was a far bigger challenge than information overload. Experts tell us that the weekend edition of the *New York Times* contains more information than the average person in the 17th century would have come across during their entire lifetime!

That's a pretty amazing fact until you stop to realize that it means the Information Age is just starting out in life. It isn't even an adolescent yet. In fact, it's only an infant!... and it's growing faster than baby Godzilla!

> *The choice of books, like that of friends, is a serious duty. We are as responsible for what we read as what we do.*
>
> —John Lubbock

Explosion on the Internet

Consider this: It took radio 38 years to reach 50 million listeners. It took TV 13 years to reach that mark. It only took the Internet four years to attract 50 million users!

As I write this, the Internet connects 175 million users online, 100 million people in the U.S. and Canada alone. The IDC, an Internet research firm, predicts there will be 320 million users online by 2002, and by 2010, the Internet will be at the center of one billion people's lives—that's one out of every six people on earth!

This means that one-sixth of the world's population will have immediate, inexpensive access to libraries... museums... websites... businesses... scientific research... and individuals all over the world—and that's only the tip of the iceberg! The body of information on the Internet *is doubling every six months*!

Talk about the information explosion. We're eye witnesses to the detonation of the Internet bomb—the I-bomb, I call it! The I-bomb is to the Information Age what the A-bomb was to WWII—the end-all and be-all! And before it's all over, the fall-out from the I-bomb's growing mushroom cloud will touch billions of people all over the globe.

Dummying Down the Media

The information explosion means that the *quantity of information* is increasing at an astronomical rate. But what about the *quality of information?* If we're getting more information, can we also say it's getting better?

In a word, no. Make that a capital NO (with an exclamation mark)!

Tragically, there's an inverse proportion between the *quantity* of information available to us and the *quality* of that information. Here's why.

> *If we encountered a man of rare intellect, we should ask him what books he read.*
>
> *—Emerson*

The Internet came out of nowhere and captured 175 million users in a few short years. As a result of the Internet's increasing popularity, the big three media industries—TV, radio, and newspapers—are losing customers hand over fist. TV watching is down as much as 28% in some markets. Radio listening is down 18%. Daily newspaper circulations have dropped 66% since 1950, and revenues from classified ads, which make up a big portion of a newspaper's income, are dropping like a brick.

Now, let me ask you a question: Do you think the big wigs at ABC, Turner Broadcasting, and the *New York Times* are going to roll over and play dead while the Internet eats their lunch?

Not a chance.

They're fighting back the only way they know how—by appealing to our basest instincts. They figure the only way to stand out from the competition is to get louder, lewder, and cruder than the next guy. So they just keep "dummying down" their programming by pushing the standards lower and lower. The result is trash TV symbolized by *The Jerry Springer Show*... "shock jocks" like Howard Stern... tabloid journalism... celebrity worship... sexploitation and "slasher" movies... increasing nudity and controversy in advertising... and far-out publicity stunts.

Does anyone really care that Dennis Rodman puts on a wedding dress and marries himself? Then why is it on the front page of every newspaper in the country? Why does Barbara Walters interview the guy on TV? Why does Hollywood give him millions of bucks to appear in a movie? Why does a major publisher advance him millions for his "autobiography" (which, by the way, he said he never read even though he was supposed to have written it. Go figure!). Why all the media attention? Because Dennis Rodman is loud, lewd, and crude, and the mass media knows that loud, lewd, and crude sells.

That is, it sells if people buy it.

And folks, I'm not buying it.

It's garbage. And I don't choose to buy garbage. I choose to throw the garbage out.

Garbage In, Garbage Out

There's an expression that originated in the computer industry—*garbage in, garbage out*—that also applies to us humans as we attempt to sort through the info-glut and identify the information that can be useful to us.

Garbage in, garbage out means the output from a computer is only as good as the input. If someone enters the data incorrectly into a computer, then the printout will reflect the mistakes. "Garbage in, garbage out."

> *A man only learns by two things; One is reading and the other is association with smarter people.*
>
> *—Will Rogers*

The same goes for humans. People who read weekly tabloids to learn the latest gossip about Hollywood celebrities or who spend hours watching re-runs on TV are filling their hearts and minds with garbage. "Garbage in, garbage out" means that humans will think and act according to the information they take in. If you take in negative, mean-spirited language and a cynical view of the world, you'll speak and act accordingly. In short, you are what you watch... you are what you listen to... you are what you read.

Screening Out the Bad Information

The danger in the Information Age is that we spend too much of our time gathering useless or harmful information rather than information that can help us grow. If you are serious about growing rich in all areas of your life, you have to start screening out the info-garbage and feeding yourself positive, uplifting messages. You can't just read anything and grow rich!

So what's the answer? The first step is awareness. We need to be alert to the problem of data smog and make a conscious effort to screen the bad information from the good. We have to be vigilant and avoid falling for the glitz... the gossip... the grunge... and the garbage. David Shenk, author of *Data Smog—Surviving the Information Glut*, suggests a bold solution to the problem of how to screen out negative messages while allowing the positive ones to filter through:

> *It took radio 38 years to reach 50 million listeners. It took TV 13 years to reach that mark. It only took the Internet four years to attract 50 million users.*

"Cancel your cable TV service, ... and apply the same [money] per month to one or more good books. Books are the opposite of television: They are slow, engaging, inspiring, intellect-rousing, and creativity-spurring."

"You could also consider limiting yourself to no more than a certain number of hours on the Internet each week, or at least balancing the amount of time spent online with an equal amount of time reading books."

Shenk's heart is in the right place, but, frankly, I think his solution to data smog is too unrealistic. As I've said before, TV isn't all bad. (And besides, every TV set I've ever seen has an on-off switch. More people need to use the "off switch" more often.) Rather than canceling our TV service, we need to discipline ourselves to watch programs that build us up, rather than tear us down.

As for reducing time on the Internet, I say it all depends on what you're doing on the Internet. Like TV, the Internet isn't all good or all bad. The good or bad comes from how we use it. If we use the Internet to read and grow rich, well, frankly, I can't think of a better medium, for the information available on the Internet can make you rich indeed—both literally and figuratively!

A Case for Guided Reading

I truly believe that 'most people want to improve their lives. They want to grow richer in all areas of their lives. They just don't know where to start. I believe that more people would read positive, uplifting books if they knew which books to read and where to get them.

That's the beauty of belonging to a reading group or a book-of-the-month club. Someone with knowledge and experience will guide you through the info-glut by selecting books for you to read. In return, you get access to information that can improve and enhance your life—in short, information that can make you richer.

There are scores of book-of-the-month clubs out there tailored to different needs. There are at least a dozen major book-of-the-month clubs and hundreds, perhaps thousands, of smaller ones. There are history book-of-the-month clubs. Religious clubs. Sports... art... biographies... literature... WWII... cooking... personal growth—you name the subject, and there's probably a book-of-the-month club available.

> *"If I could give young people one piece of advice, it would be read, read, read! In reading you will open up new worlds, real and imagined. Read for information, read for pleasure. Our libraries are filled with knowledge and joy, and it's all there—free for the taking.*
>
> —Abigail Van Buren

Big corporations are even jumping on the book-of-the-month band wagon. IBM started a voluntary book club called the North American Sales Center Book Club. "We want to be a learning organization, and the book club is one step toward that goal," says an IBM manager.

Perhaps the most famous book club in America—Oprah Winfrey's Book Club—isn't really a book club at all. It's more of a recommended reading program. But when Oprah tells her dedicated, worldwide audience of 20 million people to buy a book, half a million copies fly off the shelves in a matter of days.

A lifelong reader, Oprah is a living testimony to the power

of reading, and her book club is part of her larger vision to elevate the standards of daytime TV. She calls her latest programming concept "Change Your Life TV," and the book-of-the-month concept dovetails perfectly into her self-help philosophy of life.

Change Your Life by Reading

Abigail Van Buren, better known to most people as "Dear Abby," started writing her popular advice column when Oprah Winfrey was only two years old. In the days when fewer than one out of 10 Americans even owned a TV set, Dear Abby was syndicated in newspapers across this country, and she's long been an advocate of less TV and more reading.

Books are the opposite of television: They are slow, engaging, inspiring, intellect-rousing, and creativity-spurring.

—David Shenk

Here's her advice to young people about the importance of reading. For that matter, her words are great advice for people of any age.

f I could give young people one piece of advice, it would be read, read, read! In reading you will open up new worlds, real and imagined. Read for information, read for pleasure. Our libraries are filled with knowledge and joy, and it's all there—free for the taking. The person who does not read is no better off than the person who cannot read

"Read, read, read!" Wise words from a wise woman. No wonder her advice column has lasted more than 40 years....

11

The Reading Explosion

A room without books is like
a body without a soul.

—Cicero

HAVE YOU EVER BEEN INSIDE a Barnes & Noble or Borders superstore? *They're humongus!* You could fit 10 regular-sized bookstores in one of those places and have room left over for a small gymnasium.

Barnes & Noble and Borders have built nearly 1,000 of these mega-bookstores across the U.S. and Canada, and both companies are still in a major expansion mode. These two industry giants plan on doubling their retail space in the coming decade; Barnes & Noble is planning to open 90 new superstores a year and Borders 40.

Why the big expansion push? Both Barnes & Noble and Borders understand that lots of books equals lots of bucks. By building superstores and buying up smaller chains, these two rivals are staking their claim to a $30 billion-a-year industry

---

that is growing at a rate of 8% a year.

According to the American Booksellers Association, book sales in the U.S. grew from $18 billion in 1992... to $27 billion in 1997 (on sales of 2.1 billion books) ... and is predicted to reach $35 billion in the year 2002. *That translates to a 100% increase in sales in only 10 years, folks...* and that's big opportunity—and big business—by anyone's yardstick!

In this chapter we're going to take a closer look at the reading explosion to see who the players are... how books are sold... who's buying them... how technology is changing our reading habits... and why those who can't read, or won't read, are destined to get left behind.

Let's start with some statistics that are sure to surprise you.

Booming Sales in Book-of-the-Month Clubs

You might think the superstores would dominate book sales, what with their deep discounts and huge selections (some superstores have more than 250,000 different titles available on the floor). But that's not the case. According to the Book Industry Study Group, the big chain stores account for only about 25% of book sales. Independent bookstores account for another 15%. That means only 40% of all books sold in North America are purchased through bookstores.

> *Of making many books there is no end.*
> —Ecclesiastes

Simple math tells us that 60% of the books sold every year are sold outside of bookstores. Can you guess the biggest outlet for non-bookstore sales? Here's a hint: One out of every six books sold in this country is moved through this distribution channel. Give up?

The answer is *book-of-the-month clubs*!

Who would have guessed that 20% of all books sold outside of bookstores would be sold through book-of-the-month clubs? Not me, for one. Before I became an avid reader, I used to think book-of-the-month club members were either nerds or retired folks with too much time on their hands. Nothing could be further from the truth.

Rescued by a Book of the Month

Book-of-the-month clubs are mostly made up of eager, vibrant people of all ages and backgrounds seeking to read and grow rich or searching for answers.

One of the biggest services book-of-the-month clubs provide their members is what I call "guided reading." In effect, book-of-the-month clubs serve the same function as search engines on the Internet—they sort through info-glut and identify the material that can help their readers grow personally... professionally... and spiritually.

I'd like to share a couple true stories with you about two friends of mine whose lives were dramatically changed by guided reading in a book-of-the-month club. The first story is about a guy named Pat. Pat was an ambitious, hard-working father of three who appeared to have it all. He lived in a big house and pulled down some big

> *The new source of power is not money in the hands of a few but information in the hands of many.*
>
> —John Naisbitt

bucks working 70 hours a week as the service director of a Nissan dealership. On the outside he appeared to have it all. But on the inside, Pat was churning. Something was missing in his life. He wasn't happy, but he couldn't quite put his finger on the source of his discontent.

Pat joined a business that offered a book-of-the-month club featuring personal growth books. The first book he received was Og Mandino's *The Choice*. Pat opened the book and began to read. Two hours later he was staring straight ahead into space, the completed book in his lap.

"That book is about me," he thought to himself. "My home is a hotel. My work is my life. I never see my kids. My priorities are all out of whack. This is crazy!"

One single book opened Pat's eyes to the realities of his life. And he didn't like what he saw. Within months Pat resigned from his job of 17 years to pursue a long-denied dream—owning his own business. He became an avid reader of personal growth books, working his way through most of Mandino's books plus a score of others. The more books he read, the more enlightened he became. As a result, Pat rearranged his priorities to put his family first and expanded his personal vision of who he was and what he could become. Today he owns two growing businesses and "greets each day with love in his heart," to paraphrase his mentor, Og Mandino.

From a Wretch to a Writer

The second story is about Jim, and it illustrates the magical transformative power of reading even more than Pat's story.

The illiterate of the future will not be the person who cannot read. It will be the person who does not know how to learn.

—Alvin Toffler

If you knew Jim 10 years ago, you'd be amazed at how far he's come in his life. Fact is, you'd be amazed Jim was still alive!

You see, 10 years ago Jim was living in a flophouse in New York City, existing on mayonnaise sandwiches, two packs of cigarettes, and a quart of cheap vodka a day. He always walked the streets with his head down, scanning the sidewalk for loose change or a half-smoked cigarette. Jim's self-esteem was in the gutter. He was soaked to the soul in self-loathing, and he continued to berate his self-esteem by telling himself he deserved the head-splitting hangovers... he deserved the smoker's cough... he deserved the bleeding gums that come from a bad diet.

Now, let me interrupt Jim's story to tell you that the Jim I know was never deserving of any of these self abuses. He's one of the gentlest, kindest, most sincere people I've ever known. And I'm sure he wasn't much different 10 years ago. But when a man's self-esteem is in the gutter, he doesn't see that side of himself. All Jim saw at the time was a hopeless drunk. He hated himself for his weakness, so he beat himself up with the bottle every waking hour.

Jim was watching a bad movie on late-night TV in a five-dollar-a-night flophouse when he hit bottom. His self-loathing was complete. He knew he couldn't sink any lower. With tears streaming down his cheeks, he begged God to help him climb out of the pit of self-hatred. That night Jim began the long, painful journey back from the brink of despair. The next day he attended an Alcoholic's Anonymous meeting. Within a week he landed his first full-time job.

Over the next few years, Jim read every book on positive thinking he could get his hands on. He joined a book-of-the-month club specializing in personal growth books, and over the next few years he devoured books by the masters, writers like Dr. Norman Vincent Peale... Dr. Robert Schuller... Napoleon Hill... and Dale Carnegie. Jim began to keep a journal, writing down his innermost feelings and his daily reflections on what he'd read.

> *Gutenberg made everybody a reader. Xerox makes everybody a publisher.*
>
> —Marshall McLuhan

Gradually, Jim began to heal. Through his daily readings and reflections, the anger melted away. The self-contempt faded. The doubts and fears subsided. He began to recognize his self-worth. He began to reach out to others who were struggling with their own lives through his speeches and writings.

Just 10 years ago, Jim had hit bottom. But he climbed out of his pit of self-despair on a stairway built out of books. He wasn't the first person to rescue himself through reading. And he won't be the last. His life is proof that guided reading can enlighten us and point the way to self-awareness... contentment... wholeness... and happiness.

Who Is Reading—and Why?

To no one's surprise, college-educated adults are the most avid readers. Recognizing this demographic, Barnes & Noble won't even consider opening a new superstore unless there are 25,000 college graduates living within a 10- to 15-mile radius of the site.

High school graduates, on the other hand, are less likely to be avid readers than college graduates. In fact, 37% of all high school graduates never read a book after high school, and half of all Americans read one book every 10 years, regardless of their education level. The age group that reads the most are the 45-55 year olds, followed by the 30-44 year olds, which is understandable given the fact that 30 to 55 are the peak years for earning and personal growth.

So what do these statistics tell us? I can't speak for you, but the statistics tell me that reading is more a matter of choice than chance. In other words, there's a big difference between *being able to read* and *choosing to read*! The truth is the statistics don't mean much when you take each individual into account.

> *If you want to be successful, you have to do what successful people do. And one of the things successful people do is read and grow rich.*
>
> —Burke Hedges

Just because the average person in this country only reads one book every 10 years doesn't mean YOU can't read more books than that, isn't that true? (As I pointed out earlier, if you had been reading only 15 minutes a day, you could have read 120 books during that 10-year period.)

The fact that you have a high school diploma or a college diploma doesn't *cause* you to read more or less—*only YOU can cause you to read more or less*! All I can tell you for sure is this. People who want to grow, no matter what their age, background, or education level, will find excuses TO read, instead of finding excuses NOT TO read. You can choose to be the exception and become an avid reader just as easily as you can choose to be the rule and remain a non-reader.

Fact is, there are thousands of people representing each age group and education level who are *choosing to read*. And there are thousands of others representing the same age groups and education levels who are *choosing not to read*. In the end, the demographic you are part of doesn't choose you—*you choose your demographic*!

Like I always tell people at my seminars, "If you want to be successful, you have to do what successful people do." And one of the things successful people do is read and grow rich.

Back to the Future of Books

Up to this point we've talked a lot about the recent changes going on in the book industry, most especially changes in how books are published and sold. But the one constant through all these changes is the format of the book itself. For the most part, books today still look like they did when they were first invented centuries ago. But that's about to change. There's a new kind of book being introduced into the marketplace called an "e-book"—and it could dramatically change the way we buy and read books in the coming years.

To better understand the future of books, let's take a moment to talk about how books originated. What we call books— that is, bound pages printed on both sides—came about centuries after the invention of writing. Most of the earliest known documents were written on large scrolls made from papyrus (from which the word "paper" is derived) or animal skins.

Books originated with the early Christians, who wanted to study Scripture but could not worship openly for fear of persecution. They couldn't risk carrying around large scrolls, so they started looking for ways to conceal letters and teachings from the New Testament. Some resourceful soul came up with the idea of cutting blank scrolls into smaller sections or "pages" and then folding each page in half twice. By cutting along the edge of the bottom fold, the folded page was transformed into a booklet with eight pages, front and back. These booklets could easily be hidden inside a robe.

Flash forward 2,000 years to your computer screen. Compare the sophisticated technology of computers to the early books. A bright, smooth computer screen replaces the rough, dried papyrus. Electronic images replace hand-drawn letters. And the scroll replaces the pages of a book.

WHAT? Did you say scroll? I thought scrolls were replaced by books centuries ago! Ah, irony of ironies—20 centuries of "progress," and we return to the old, awkward medium we thought we'd left behind forever—we access text on the computer screen by scrolling!

E-Gads! E-Books!

The latest breakthrough in reading technology is the electronic book—"e-book" for short. E-books are a hybrid of a traditional book and a computer, and the battery-powered models currently available weigh several pounds and look like small lap-top computers minus the keyboard. Prices range from $300 to more than $2,000 for the e-book itself, and customers will be charged additional money for the content.

America Online signed up 35 million subscribers in less than six years—that's more subscribers than "Newsweek", "Time", and "US News & World Report" combined!

To buy content, such as a book or magazine, you would plug your e-book into a personal computer connected to the Internet. You would access an online bookstore, which would download the content onto your e-book for a fee. Once you paid for your content, you would own it forever. A record of your purchase would remain on file with the seller in the event you wanted to download your book in the future.

In the long run, the key issue isn't the format of a book. The issue is *how much* people are reading and *what* they are choosing to read. With the dynamic growth of the Internet, it's a foregone conclusion that much of our reading will be done off a monitor.

In the time it takes to read this paragraph, for example, there will be a million e-mail messages sent—and that's a trend that will only increase. America Online signed up 35 million subscribers in less than six years—that's more subscribers than *Newsweek, Time,* and *US News & World Report* combined! No question that e-reading is here to stay. That's just a fact. Like I said, the issue isn't the medium of the written word. The issue is whether you are choosing to be a reader or a non-reader.

Get on Board the Reading Bus

When I talk about reading or non-reading being a matter of choice, it reminds me of the story about a baseball manager who became increasingly frustrated with his team's prolonged losing streak. The best hitters were in a slump. The most reliable infielders were making costly errors. And all of the players were bickering and pointing fingers at one another. Team morale was at an all-time low.

The manager had seen and heard enough. It was time for the players to get back to the basics by putting in some extra practice. He decided to give the players a choice. They could either get to the ballpark early and get in some extra practice, or they could stay at the hotel until game time. Here's how he worded his notice to the players:

Tomorrow there will be two buses leaving the hotel for the ballpark. The two o'clock bus will be for those who need a little extra work. The empty bus will be leaving at five o'clock.

The players got the point. All of them were early for the two o'clock bus.

This cute story makes a very serious point. If we want better results, we have to choose to "get on the bus" so that we can practice the things that make us better. We can also choose NOT to practice, but that choice has dire consequences that can lead to certain failure. That's why I always tell people, "For things to get better, YOU have to get better. For things to change, YOU have to change."

For baseball players, getting better starts with getting on the "practice bus." For the rest of us, getting better starts with getting on the "reading bus."

The passengers on the "reading bus" will be on their way to more abundance ... more fulfillment... more happiness... in short, more of everything they want out of life. The non-readers, on the other hand, will be left behind at the bus terminal, angry and confused, wondering why they're stuck in the same old rut.

I chose to board the reading bus years ago.

And there's a lot of great company on board.

I just wish there weren't so many empty seats....

12

Personal Growth Books Hall of Fame: a Brief Survey of the Most Influential Personal Growth Books Ever Written

*There's only one corner of the universe
you can be certain of improving
and that's your own self.*

–Aldous Huxley

HAVE YOU SEEN THE HIT MOVIE, *You've Got Mail*, starring Tom Hanks and Meg Ryan? It's a cute story that captures the growing tension between the giant Barnes & Noble-type bookstore chains and the small, independent bookstores.

The lead female character, played by Ryan, owns a small children's bookstore, while Hanks' family owns a nearby superstore that is driving Ryan out of business. To Hanks, books are a business. To Ryan, books are a way of life. At one point Ryan gushes that she loves what she does, and Hanks asks her what's so special about selling books to little kids.

"I love what I do because books tell children who they are long before they ever become it," she replies sincerely.

Isn't that a wonderful line? It pretty well sums up the power of reading to shape young lives. In fact, it sums up the power of reading to shape our lives at any age. The way I see it, Ryan's comment applies to personal growth books just as much as it applies to children's books. Personal growth books tell us who we can become before we become it. They give us hope. They stir our imagination. They inspire us to take action. They make us stretch ourselves. They plant the seeds that grow and blossom into our dreams. They challenge us to live up to our full potential. In short, they empower us to change... to get better... to grow rich.

Personal Growth Books Dominate Bestseller Lists

Personal growth books go by a lot of different names—motivational books... inspirational books... self-help books... self-improvement books... people skills books... success principle books... well, you get the idea. I prefer to use the term "personal growth books" because their purpose is to help people grow richer in the largest sense of the word—richer in relationships... in money... in happiness... in fulfillment... in purpose, and so on.

> *Whatever reason you had for not being somebody, there's somebody who had the same problem and overcame it.*
>
> —Barbara Reynolds

Fifty years ago there were only a handful of personal growth books available. But today the personal growth industry has exploded into a half billion-dollar-a-year industry. Most people aren't satisfied with settling for less these days. They understand that "pursuing happiness" means pursuing their full potential, and millions of North Americans are seeking to grow richer in their lives by reading.

A 1999 article in *USA Today* compiled a list of the top 100 bestselling books over the last five years. Guess how many of the top 10 bestsellers were personal growth books? One? Two? TRY NINE!

That's right—nine of the top 10 bestselling books over a five-year period were personal growth books, led by *Men Are From Mars, Women Are From Venus* at number one, followed by *Don't Sweat the Small Stuff...* at number two and *Chicken Soup for the Soul* at three.

The only fiction book to crack the top 10 was John Grisham's *The Chamber*, at number 10. Fully one-third of the top 100 bestsellers were personal growth books! *Chicken Soup for the Soul* led the way with six different versions in the top 100. Americans shelled out $538 million for personal growth books in 1997, according to Simba, a research firm in Stamford, Connecticut, and consumers spend more money on books each year than they do on videos, CDs, daily newspapers, and magazines.

Famous People Who Have Read & Grown Rich

I'm a champion of personal growth books because I know firsthand how they can change lives. "I'm a product of the product," as they say. A personal growth book inspired me to change my life 180 degrees, and books continue to enrich my life on a daily basis.

But I'm not the only person whose life has been changed dramatically by a personal growth book, that's for sure! Scores of famous people point to a personal growth book as the turning point in their lives, including these household names:

> *The average salesman doesn't read a book a year. That is why he is the average salesman.*
>
> —Anonymous

- **Lou Holtz**, one of the winningest coaches in college football history, credits *The Magic of Thinking Big* as a turning point in his professional career.
- **W. Clement Stone**, multi-millionaire businessman and bestselling author, says that Napoleon Hill's *Think and Grow Rich* "changed the course of my life." Hill's book inspired Stone to begin a lifelong habit of helping others by giving them personal growth books, a habit he followed religiously for 50 years.
- **Donna Reed**, Academy Award-winner and early TV star, was a shy, insecure high school freshman when she read *How to Win Friends and Influence People*. Upon completing the book, she landed a lead role in the school play, setting the stage for a 40-year career in movies and TV.

- **J.W. Marriott**, president of Marriott Hotels, was so moved by the message of *The Greatest Salesman in the World* that he gives a copy to each of his marketing executives.
- **Les Brown** was labeled "mentally handicapped" in middle school and was on the verge of dropping out when he accidently heard a recording of Earl Nightingale's *The Strangest Secret*. The message inspired Brown to work harder and think more positively, and today he's one of the most sought-after motivational speakers in the country.
- **Phyllis Diller**, the famous comedienne, was a frustrated, insecure housewife when she read *The Magic of Believing*. The book gave her the confidence to try her hand at show business, and she went on to become one of the best-known comics in the country.
- **Archie Moore**, the former light-heavyweight boxing champion who knocked out a record 141 opponents in 228 bouts, wasn't much of a reader until he was cast as the slave Jim in the movie version of *The Adventures of Huckleberry Finn*. Moore read the book to prepare himself for the part and from then on became an avid reader, saying, "Now that I've found books, I'm really living."
- **Dave Thomas**, founder of Wendy's Restaurants, was a high school dropout with a low self-concept when he happened to read *The Power of Positive Thinking*. Today he heads up a fast-food empire with thousands of restaurants all over the world.
- **Oprah Winfrey**, talk show host, actor, and producer, credits her incredible success to books: "I can't imagine I could have become the person I am now without books. How would I know there was another world beyond my small, isolated, feeling-abandoned world? Books became synonymous with freedom. They showed that you can open doors and walk through."

These are but a few of the thousands of stories of men and women who were inspired by a book to seek higher levels of achievement, proving that Roy L. Smith was right on the mark when he observed that "some good book is usually responsible for the success of every really great man."

What It Means to Be a Classic

The personal growth movement has really caught fire over the last decade or so, and today there are scores of first-rate books that can help people to read and grow rich. But let's face it, only a few are worthy of being called a classic. Just as there have been thousands of talented men to play major league baseball, only the best of the best have been inducted into the Major League Baseball Hall of Fame. The Hall is reserved for the legends—Babe Ruth... Mickey Mantle... Hank Aaron. The players in the Hall of Fame earned their honor because they consistently performed on a level far above average. They innovated. They redefined the way the game is played. And because of their exceptional play, they set new standards for the players who followed.

The same can be said for a handful of personal growth books. They broke new ground. They challenged the way we think of ourselves and the world. And they inspired generations of readers to higher levels of achievement. These are the classics—the personal growth books that have passed the test of time... the books that have inspired millions of people all over the world to change their lives for the better.

> *A man's reading program should be as carefully planned as his daily diet, for that too is food, without which he cannot grow mentally.*
>
> —Andrew Carnegie

All of the writings in the Personal Growth Books Hall of Fame are still in print, even though five of them were first published more than a century ago. All but two of the books were written by Americans, an understandable phenomenon given this country's youthful spirit and can-do attitude. They've all sold well over a million copies and have been translated into scores of foreign languages (several titles have been translated into 50 or more foreign languages). And most of the books continue to sell upwards of 100,000 a year, year in and year out.

What follows is a list of the books in my Personal Growth

Books Hall of Fame. I've chosen to list them according to
date of publication so that you can better understand the role
each book played in the history of the personal growth movement.

The Personal Growth Books Hall of Fame

1. *Pilgrim's Progress*, John Bunyan (1670)
John Bunyan, a fiery minister and outspoken critic of the
Church of England, wrote *Pilgrim's Progress* during one of his
long stays in prison. The forerunner to the English novel,
Bunyan's entertaining allegory could be considered the first
personal growth book outside the Bible. Bunyan's story
chronicles the adventures of a young hero, Christian, on his
travels to salvation. Christian encounters many obstacles on
his journey, including the Hill of Difficulty... the Valley of
Humiliation... and the Giant of Despair in Doubting Castle.
Pilgrim's Progress teaches readers many of the key principles
necessary for success and personal growth, such as persistence,
discipline, integrity, focus, belief, and commitment. *Pilgrim's
Progress* shaped the values of many great leaders, including
Benjamin Franklin and Abraham Lincoln.

2. *Autobiography of Benjamin Franklin* (1793)
Franklin was one of the first American success stories, a poor
boy with little formal education who became a "self-made man"
through hard work and owning his own business. Franklin
was a tireless promoter of self improvement, and one of his
earliest publications, *Poor Richard's Almanack*, offered inspiring stories, clever proverbs, and commonsense advice on how
to get ahead in life. Although Franklin only attended two
years of school, he became one of the most educated men of
his time by reading widely in classic literature, science, politics, and philosophy. He started the first lending library in
the country as an inexpensive way for poor people to educate
and improve themselves, just as he had done. His autobiography is just as readable and entertaining as it was when it was
first written more than 200 years ago, and it provides wonderful insights into one of history's most versatile and innovative
thinkers.

3. Essays by Ralph Waldo Emerson and Henry David Thoreau (1840s)

Emerson's essay, *Self Reliance*, and Thoreau's essay, *Walden*, are required reading in every high school in America—and for good reason. Emerson and Thoreau epitomized the American spirit of individualism and self-determination. Their essays were full of optimism, urging readers to trust their intuition... to shape their destiny... to follow their dreams... to realize their fullest potential... to discover their ultimate purpose in life. Their powerful, original writings advocated the concepts that represent the underpinnings of the personal growth movement, such as positive thinking... a can-do spirit... going against the grain... being your own person... and making things happen. In short, the writings of Emerson and Thoreau shaped our national character and defined what it is to be an American.

4. Horatio Alger Stories (1860-1899)

Horatio Alger wrote more than 100 books (several of which are still in publication) for children and young adults in which the heroes rise from poverty to prosperity through discipline, integrity, good deeds, and hard work. Today the term "Horatio Alger story" is part of our vocabulary, often used to describe a true-to-life "rags to riches story" about someone who overcomes tremendous odds to achieve success. It is estimated that Alger's books, including the *Ragged Dick* and *Tattered Tom* series, sold more than 20 million copies in his lifetime, inspiring millions of young people from the wrong side of the tracks to reach for the stars.

5. *Acres of Diamonds*, Russell Conwell (1890s)

In the late 1800s, Russell Conwell, a minister and founder of Temple University, traveled the country raising funds for the university and various causes by giving a speech he called *Acres of Diamonds*, the story of an ambitious young man in Persia who sells his farm and travels the continent searching for diamonds. The man searches in vain for years but to no avail. Sick, broke, and disillusioned, he drowns himself. Meanwhile, the farm's new owner accidently discovers his land is covered with "acres of diamonds!" The story points out that every man and woman could attain great wealth if they would only look for the opportunities in their own back yard. The key to riches is to find out what other people around us need and then to fulfill those needs. Rev. Conwell read his essay more than 6,000 times to packed audiences during his lifetime, and it has been reproduced in print and audio and circulated to millions of people over the last century.

6. *As a Man Thinketh*, James Allen (1910)

James Allen was a 38-year-old middle manager in a factory when he retired in order to discover the secret to happiness and then teach it to others through his writings. Allen wrote 19 books during the last nine years of his life, the most famous being *As a Man Thinketh*, which takes its title from the proverbs of King Solomon, who said, "As a man thinketh in his heart, so is he." Allen is considered the "granddaddy" of modern inspirational literature, and his thesis that "before you can change your life, you have to change your thoughts" remains one of the dominant themes in the personal growth movement.

7. *How to Win Friends and Influence People*, Dale Carnegie (1937)

Dale Carnegie taught courses on public speaking and the art of getting along with others to professionals and businessmen for 25 years before compiling his teachings into one of the bestselling personal growth books in history. To date the book has sold nearly 20 million copies and has been translated into every major language in the world. Carnegie writes in a very conversational style and offers timeless, common-sense tips on how to win people over to your point of view, including chapters on how to make a good first impression... an easy way to become a good conversationalist... how to criticize and not be hated for it... and how to spur people on to success. *How to Win Friends and Influence People* is in a class by itself!

8. *Think & Grow Rich*, Napoleon Hill (1937)

Napoleon Hill interviewed more than 500 of the nation's most successful businessmen in an effort to come up with a success formula the average man could follow. Hill distilled the wisdom from the legends of the Industrial Age—including Ford, Carnegie, Rockefeller, Edison, Wrigley, Firestone, and Woolworth, to name a few—into the essential principles for wealth creation. The book was an instant success when it was first published in the midst of the Great Depression and has sold upwards of 20 million copies over the years. More than 60 years after its publication, *Think & Grow Rich* is still the first and finest book ever written about the "secrets" to achieving financial independence. For people who are serious about creating more wealth for themselves and their family, this personal growth classic is a must read.

9. *The Power of Positive Thinking*, Dr. Norman Vincent Peale (1952)

Dr. Peale's book is likely the most famous personal growth book in history, and the phrase "the power of positive thinking" has become an everyday expression and a rallying call for optimists all over the world. The book offers practical advice to "the plain people in life" to help them face their problems and go on to lead "a happy, satisfying, and worthwhile life." A blend of common sense, research, psychology, and Scripture, *The Power of Positive Thinking* offers practical advice on how to deal successfully with everyday problems, such as how to break the worry habit... how to get people to like you... how to relax... how to have constant energy... how to create your own happiness. Dr. Peale gave several speeches a week all across the country and preached three sermons every Sunday at the Marble Collegiate Church of New York City until he was well into his 90s, proving once and for all the veracity of his simple, yet profound, philosophy of living.

10. *The Strangest Secret*, Earl Nightingale (1956)

Originally written as an essay, Earl Nightingale's recording of the *Strangest Secret* became the first non-musical recording to sell over a million copies. Nightingale enjoyed a 40-year career as a speaker and announcer in radio and TV, and he hosted more than 7,000 broadcasts on his popular radio program, *Our Changing World*, where he would read inspirational stories and poems while classical music played in the background. *The Strangest Secret*, however, remained Nightingale's signature piece, and its essential message that "you are a sum total of what you think about all day long" has become a major theme in almost every personal growth book written in the last 50 years, a lasting tribute to Nightingale's classic essay.

11. *The Magic of Thinking Big*, David J. Schwartz, Ph.D. (1959)

Dr. Schwartz's book drives home the message that the size of a person's success is directly proportional to the size of their thinking. In Schwartz's words, "Case history after case history proved that the size of bank accounts, the size of happiness accounts, and the size of one's general satisfaction account is dependent on the size of one's thinking." *The Magic of Thinking Big* is perhaps the easiest-reading personal growth book ever written. The language is simple and conversational, the information is practical, and anecdotes and stories are sprinkled throughout every page, making the reading fun and entertaining.

12. *Psycho-Cybernetics*, Maxwell Maltz (1960)

Don't let the academic-sounding title scare you—*Psycho-Cybernetics* is anything but a stuffy college textbook! Dr. Maltz was a plastic surgeon who became fascinated with the way some of his patients' self-image improved after cosmetic surgery, while others continued to think of themselves as inferior or even "ugly" despite their improved looks. Dr. Maltz surmised that our self-image has a "face" too, and that by altering our self-image we can alter our personality and behavior. Our self-image sets the boundaries of what we think we can accomplish, so by altering our self-image, we can expand "our areas of possibility." *Psycho-Cybernetics* offers many techniques that will help you improve your self-image, with chapters on how to acquire the habit of happiness... how to remove emotional scars... and how to turn crisis into creative opportunity.

13. *The Greatest Salesman in the World*, Og Mandino (1968)

Mandino does a brilliant job of giving dignity and respect to the ancient profession of selling, which has been maligned and misunderstood by all too many people. Mandino's extended parable seems simple and direct, but the story turns out to be deceptively profound, for the author uses several clever plot twists to teach readers the 10 key principles that will empower them to become successful in sales and in life. The book will surprise you... entertain you... inspire you... teach you... and delight you. It's short enough to read in an hour or two, but the messages will stay with you for a lifetime. The *Greatest Salesman in the World* is proof that big things come in small packages.

Honorable Mention:
- *Man's Search for Meaning*, Dr. Viktor Frankl (1959)
- *7 Habits of Highly Effective People*, Dr. Steven Covey (1989)
- *Chicken Soup for the Soul*, Jack Canfield and
    Mark Victor Hansen (1993)
- *See You at the Top*, Zig Ziglar (1975)
- Various Books by Dr. Robert H. Schuller
- *The Magic of Believing*, Claude M. Bristol (1948)
- *The Richest Man in Babylon*, George S. Clason (1926)

The World's a Better Place

I'm sure I passed over some great books that have had a powerful impact on people's lives, and I apologize if I neglected to mention one of your favorites. But I think this list pretty much recognizes the "superstars" among the personal growth books. All totaled, they've directly touched the lives of perhaps 100 million readers, and indirectly touched the lives of millions more. And I've got to believe the world is a "kinder, gentler place" as the result of people reading these books.

If you haven't read any of the books on the list, I suggest you choose a book and make a commitment to read it. Like I said, the knowledge contained in these books has enhanced the lives of people all over the world—and it can do the same for you. The information is timeless. The techniques are proven. The principles are rock-solid. To grow richer in your life, all you have to do is invest a few hours and a few dollars by buying and reading any or all of these books. There's no time like the present to start building your own Personal Growth Books Hall of Fame.

Here's the kicker—all of this wisdom, research, and experience is available for an average cost of $10 per book! In my opinion, investing $10 in a book that can help you grow rich is the best value in the history of the world! Just think, millions of lives changed for $10 a person *when it costs as much as $10,000 a year (or more) to send a kid to college.* That's more than a bargain—that's a steal!!

Read and Grow Rich

Ross Perot, the irascible billionaire who ran for U.S. President in 1992, was famous for his folksy sayings. One of my favorite sayings of his is this one: "Just because you go out and stand in the garage doesn't make you a car." That was Perot's way of saying that there's a big difference between *pretending* to do something and actually *doing it*. Some things just can't be faked.

> *In my opinion, investing $10 in a book that can help you grow rich is the best value in the history of the world!*
> —Burke Hedges

Well, the same goes for buying personal growth books. Just because you buy a personal growth book doesn't make you a reader. There are millions of great books sold every year, but sadly, statistics show that half the books bought in this country are never read! What a waste of money. What a waste of paper. What a waste of a golden opportunity!

Folks, don't be one of the 50% who buys a book and then never reads it. You can start growing rich today if you'll only start reading the books that will help you grow in your life.

To paraphrase Ross Perot, don't just go out and stand in your library. That won't make you a reader any more than standing in the garage will make you a car. Buying exercise equipment won't give you bigger muscles. The only way to get bigger muscles is to use the equipment! Likewise, the only way to get the benefits of reading is to buy a book—and then read it!

You want to get rich? Great! Me, too! Here's how: Take a book off the shelf. Take some time out of your schedule. And then *read!*

Conclusion

Reading or Regrets — the Choice Is Yours!

Books give us wings.
  –slogan for the Center for the
  Book, Library of Congress

MY FIRST FULL-TIME JOB—as I mentioned in the introduction—was building boats. I worked in a metal building without air conditioning. The hot Florida sun would beat down on the tin roof during the summers, heating the inside to oven-like temperatures.

I spent most of my days kneeling in the hull of a boat with an electric grinder in my hand, smoothing the rough fiberglass to a polished finish. When I got home from work, the first thing I did was jump in the shower and scrub the fiberglass off my arms with a stiff brush.

I worked side-by-side with a guy named Bob, and we became pretty good friends during our two years together, working by day and drinking beer by night. Then one day I happened to read *The Greatest Salesman in the World*, and less than a month later I resigned and took a job in sales.

One summer afternoon seven years later, I dropped by the boat factory to see how things were going. Not much had changed. The sun was still beating down on the metal oven housing the workers. And Bob was still standing inside a half-finished boat with a grinder in his hands.

> *Do you know someone you'd like to change, regulate, or improve? Fine. Why not start on yourself? That's a lot more profitable than trying to improve others.*
>
> —Dale Carnegie

We reminisced about the old days and exchanged small talk as I loosened my tie. At one point I mentioned to Bob that I'd written a book. He gave me a startled look.

"You wrote a book? You? You must be kidding!" he shouted over the roaring power tools.

"No, I'm serious! In fact, I think I have a copy in the car," I said as I headed outside. "Stay right there—I'll bring you back a book."

"HEY," Bob shouted after me. "IF YOU'RE GONNA BRING ME SOMETHING, DON'T BRING ME A BOOK. BRING ME A BEER!"

The whole place broke up laughing.

Choosing to Grow

On my drive back home, I did a lot of thinking. And one of the things I kept thinking about was the power of choice. You see, seven years earlier Bob and I were in the exact same place. We worked hard. And we played hard. But one afternoon, instead of getting together with the guys and grabbing a couple of beers, I grabbed a book—something I didn't do very often in those days.

Bob, on the other hand, grabbed a beer—*just like always*.

Seven years later, I'd read scores of great personal growth books, written five books of my own, and founded and run several successful businesses.

Bob, on the other hand, still works all day in the hot Florida sun with a grinder in his hand—*just like always*.

You see, over the years I continued to read and grow rich

in many, many phases of my life.

Bob, on the other hand, stayed frozen in time. "Don't bring me a book, bring me a beer" became his mission statement in life—*just like always*.

Folks, you don't have to live your life "just like always." You can *choose* to change careers. You can *choose* to spend more time with your children. You can *choose* to stop procrastinating. You can *choose* to become a more considerate spouse.

> *Compared to what we aught to be, we are only half awake.*
>
> —Williams James

In other words, you can choose to do what millions of other people just like you have chosen to do... *you can choose to get better... you can choose to read more ... you can choose to grow!*

Everyone Needs to Read & Grow Richer

There's not a person alive who doesn't need to change their life for the better in one way or the other. Everyone—and I mean EVERYONE— needs to read and grow rich in some area of their lives.

This quote by Dr. Orison S. Marden, founder of *Success* magazine, epitomizes how books can help you improve your life by helping you grow:

> *If you are anxious to improve yourself, read books which tend to elevate your taste, refine your imagination, clarify your ambition, raise your ideals.*
>
> *Read books of power, books which stir the very depths of your being to some purpose. Read books which make you resolve to do and be a little better; to try a little harder to be somebody and to do something in the world.*
>
> *Fifteen minutes of concentrated reading every day would carry you through the great authors in about five years.*

Are you reading the kinds of books that Dr. Marden suggests you read? Are you reading at least 15 minutes a day, every single day? If the answer is "yes," congratulate yourself, for you are truly reading and growing rich in your life.

I challenge you to continue reading every single day— or to start reading every day if you're a reluctant reader. I challenge you to take Dr. Marden's advice and "... *read books which tend to elevate your taste... refine your imagination... clarify your ambition... and raise your ideals.*" If you do, the hidden powers of reading will make you grow richer in all areas of your life.

In closing, I wish you all the success you will allow yourself to have through the books you read—and always remember that when you keep reading... and keep going... *you keep growing*!